Preventing Workplace Bullying and Harassment

Hadyn Olsen

Disclaimer

Preventing Workplace Bullying and Harassment

Hadyn Olsen

CCH New Zealand Limited
PO BOX 33-270, Takapuna
Auckland 0740
Telephone: 0800 500 224
books.wolterskluwer.co.nz

Wolters Kluwer

Book Code: 10099361-0001

About Wolters Kluwer

Wolters Kluwer enables legal, tax, finance, and healthcare professionals to be more effective and efficient. We provide information, software, and services that deliver vital insights, intelligent tools, and the guidance of subject-matter experts. We create value by combining information, deep expertise, and technology to provide customers with solutions that improve their quality and effectiveness.

Professionals turn to us when they need actionable information to better serve their clients.

Wolters Kluwer. When you have to be right.

Enquiries are welcome on 0800 500 224.

A catalogue record for this book is available from the National Library of New Zealand.

ISBN (print): 978-1-77547-481-4

ISBN (eBook): 978-1-77547-482-1

Published by CCH New Zealand Limited

First published November 2022

Contents

Page

About the Author

Hadyn Olsen is a leading practitioner in New Zealand specialising in the prevention of workplace bullying and harassment. His work over 20 years has involved diverse roles in a variety of organisations, from consultant, facilitator, coach and trainer to investigator, mediator and troubleshooter. He has developed numerous workplace bullying prevention programmes and equipped managers, contact persons and others to respond effectively to concerns about workplace bullying.

Hadyn's background was in the pulp and paper industry, where he was a workplace contact person for harassment during the 1990s. He also trained as a violence prevention facilitator and then co-managed the Rotorua Violence Prevention Services, contracting to the New Zealand Department for Courts and the Department of Corrections for 12 years. His work with violent offenders led him to research into workplace bullying, and he began to focus his attentions on workplaces and how bullying affects organisations and what it takes to rehabilitate perpetrators.

In 2000 Hadyn became a sexual harassment trainer under the Sexual Harassment Prevention Network with the New Zealand Human Rights Commission. He also became an advisory member of the New Zealand Safety Council and is a current member of the International Association of Workplace Bullying and Harassment.

In 2002 Hadyn wrote the first New Zealand report into workplace bullying, entitled: "Workplace Bullying: What New Zealand Workplaces Should Know." He also set up "Workplaces Against Violence in Employment" (WAVE) under the Challenge Violence Trust, focusing on workplace bullying and harassment prevention. WAVE now operates in a standalone capacity.

Hadyn set up the first New Zealand workplace bullying helpline (0800 ZEROBULLY). This ran for 6 years in and was finally discontinued after being unable to cope with the demand.

In 2005 Hadyn wrote *Workplace Bullying: A Toolbox for Managers and Supervisors* (CCH New Zealand Ltd). This was updated in 2010. He has also written "Oh No You Don't: A Tale of Managing Workplace Bullies" and has published a journal article in the *New Zealand Journal of Human Resources Management* (NZJHRM) entitled "Beyond Definition: Moving Toward Effective Interventions that Stop Workplace Bullying".

Hadyn has been associated for many years with the Human Resources Institute of New Zealand and has assisted in the development of the WorkSafe New Zealand Guide "Preventing and Responding to Workplace Bullying 2014". He has been a conference speaker nationally and internationally, as well as working with a wide range of government and non-government organisations across New Zealand.

Although semi-retired, Hadyn continues to produce online training and offers advice to organisations. His website wave.org.nz is still active and provides a wealth of resources for enquirers.

Chapter 1

Introduction

¶1-010 Workplace bullying and harassment

Over the last 20 years Australian and New Zealand organisations have become increasingly aware of the phenomenon of workplace bullying and harassment. Many organisations have made considerable efforts to address bullying and harassment in their workplaces and have invested significantly in training and resources to prevent these psychosocial hazards.

After working as a bullying and harassment consultant throughout that period, I have learned a lot about what works and what doesn't work in organisations when it comes to addressing bullying and harassment. I have learned why some organisations are ridden with bullying and harassment and others are not. I have learned what it takes to begin to create a culture that prevents people from bullying and harassing. This book is written from experience, working with hundreds of organisations over many years.

This is a major issue for workplaces to address, and mistakes can be costly. Things can go from bad to worse in a very short time when someone says they have been bullied or harassed. Early intervention is very important. If this doesn't happen, polarisation can occur and people may become more protective, defensive and combative. These attitudes can spread through an entire workgroup, creating major disruption. For this reason, early intervention is crucial, and managers need to know what to do and how to do it.

In today's workplace people do not expect to be bullied or harassed. They expect to be able to do their jobs in a safe and secure environment. That seems like a reasonable expectation in this day and age. We value fair play.

Employers say they want to provide workplace environments that are safe and secure so that employees can do their jobs and be productive. That makes good business sense. It seems everyone claims they want to be bully and harassment free.

Despite this sentiment, bullying and harassment still occur, despite the existence of employment assistance programmes and even in organisations with good policies on bullying and harassment. This pernicious virus can work its way into the culture and infect it for years to come. When the dynamics of bullying and harassment become embedded within a workplace culture, they create a system that perpetuates itself. In the worst workplaces, people learn bullying tactics as a tool of survival, and the only way to stop being bullied is to learn to be a bigger bully.

I want to be clear that I have a bias when it comes to this issue. My bias is toward the development of a prevention culture that is led by managers and staff leaders. I believe in a whole system focus, not simplistic or reactive approaches. I have seen how the "zero tolerance" notion with its emphasis on reporting and complaints creates far more problems than it solves. I used to support the idea of zero tolerance but am now convinced we need something better than this. I believe in the fence at the top of the cliff rather than the wreck at the bottom. The fence is not a wire fence, but a human fence, and it works to prevent hazards rather than "not tolerate" them. In my view, when a formal complaint of bullying or harassment is made, it indicates there is a failure in the system. Someone has turned a blind eye and has ignored the early signs and signals.

This book is designed to be a practical handbook for managers and supervisors, who can make a difference if they have some basic knowledge and skills. Managers have a greater level of responsibility in workplaces to keep people safe from harm. Managers often find that responsibility daunting. They can shrink back and turn a blind eye, and this creates the perfect climate for bullying and harassment to thrive and grow.

What then can managers do? How can they work together to create significant change? They can start by treating bullying and harassment as hazards. This is a fundamental starting point. They can understand the dynamics associated with bullying and harassment. They can work to prevent these things rather than just not tolerating them. They can become proactive rather than just being reactive, and they can learn to respond skillfully when people ask for help. This will make a difference.

¶1-020 Common questions managers ask

I have trained and coached managers to resolve bullying and harassment situations. Overall, I have found that most managers want to stop bullying and harassment, and they don't want to be labelled as a bully.

These are the most common questions that managers and supervisors have:

- What is and isn't bullying?
- What is and isn't harassment?
- What should I do if someone tells me they are being bullied or harassed?
- How do I stop bullying and harassment if I know it's happening?
- How should I confront bullying and harassment when I see it happening?
- How should I respond if someone accuses me of being a bully?
- What can I do when the workplace culture is toxic?
- What can I do when people tell me they are being bullied and want me to do something, but they don't want me to name them?

- What can I do when I know bullying or harassment is happening in a team, but no one will speak up?
- What can I do when I am being bullied from below?

This book is designed to answer these questions and give practical advice. It will assist managers and supervisors to see through the cloudiness of bullying and find some clear harbour lights that will help them navigate effectively.

¶1-030 Bully and victim labels

There are some things that I wish to make clear from the beginning about my ways of thinking about bullying and harassment.

I prefer not to label people as bullies. It is a term that is widely overused. If I do use it, I use it sparsely. I have found most people who bully are not monsters. In my view, a bully is merely someone who demonstrates bullying behaviour at a particular time and in a particular place. No one is always a bully in every relationship and in every situation. Some people can be respectful and constructive in some relationships while being cruel and destructive in others.

I also find it concerning when people claim that an investigation has reached a finding that someone is a bully. Investigations do not determine that anyone is a bully. They neither determine someone's character, nor do they make psychological assessments. They only determine whether someone has used bullying behaviour.

In the same way, I do not generally label people as victims. This word is also overused. If someone is exposed to bullying behaviour, they are a target. They might be a resilient target, or they might be a damaged target. They might be a direct target of bullying behaviour if it was directed at them, or they might be an indirect target of bullying if they were exposed to bullying behaviour that was directed toward someone else. Every target is affected differently, and not all targets are victims.

The word "victim" is often associated with helplessness and powerlessness, and I do not believe that everyone affected by bullying or harassment is helpless and powerless. It is not beneficial to reinforce this. I believe in the innate creativity of human beings and their ability to survive and thrive, so I do not like labelling people with the term "victim".

In addition, the label is often used by perpetrators about themselves when they are confronted about their behaviour. Playing the victim is a common tactic of those who do not wish to take responsibility for their actions. It is a ploy to shift focus and avoid accountability. The focus I have is preventing bullying, not determining if someone is a bully or a victim.

I also tend to see harassment as a form of bullying. Bullying is the larger, more common phenomenon, and harassment is a subset of it. There are some differences, but they involve similar behaviours and often co-exist in a person's repertoire of behaviours. Where there is sexual or racial harassment, there is usually bullying as well.

¶1-040 The role of a manager in preventing bullying and harassment

Managers and supervisors have a critical role in the prevention of bullying and harassment. They need to understand how to identify these psychosocial hazards. They need to know how to prevent them and also how to respond when people approach them with concerns or complaints.

Unfortunately, the only thing necessary for bullying and harassment to thrive in a group, is that the manager passively colludes by allowing it to happen. Passive collusion is the most common occurrence and all it requires is that a manager does nothing: "The only thing necessary for evil to flourish is that good people do nothing."

Managing people is a challenging task at the best of times, and managers are usually chosen because they have technical ability, experience and skills in the job. Unfortunately, none of these attributes will assist managers to deal with bullying or harassment. Therefore, managers and supervisors need help. They often ask for help but do not get it. They want to know what "practicable steps" they should take to minimise, eliminate, isolate and prevent these hazards.

Here are some basic steps for managers:

Step 1: Take a stand personally

The first challenge that managers need to face if they are to be effective is to take a personal stand and support the organisation's bullying and harassment prevention policy. This should include a clear statement that every employee has a right to a safe workplace where they will not be bullied or harassed. Managers and supervisors should advocate and promote it personally. They need to speak against bullying and harassment and take all practicable steps to prevent it from happening.

Step 2: Don't bully or harass anyone yourself

Managers need to look at their own behaviour first and foremost. Do they use bullying or harassment behaviours at times? Do their direct reports see their behaviour falling below the line? If so, then it needs to change. Managers can get help if they have blind spots or patterns of behaviour that are questionable. It is hypocritical when managers take a stand against bullying and harassment and then use bullying and harassment themselves.

In particular, the most basic behaviours that managers should avoid are:

- **Displays of anger and hostility**. Yelling at people. Invading people's space. Threatening people either physically or verbally. Learn to maintain composure even when you are frustrated.
- **Verbal abuse and derogatory language**. Swearing at people. Using put-downs and insults. Calling people derogatory names. Publicly humiliating people and criticising them in front of others. Treat everyone with a basic level of respect, even if you personally dislike them. Be professional.
- **Abuses of power.** Being overbearing. Picking on people you don't like. Applying different standards or treating people unfairly or differently. Setting people up to fail. Be fair and be reasonable.
- **Actions that undermine.** Bad-mouthing people. Spreading malicious gossip. Having favourites and enemies within the team. Playing people off against each other. Support the success of your people and enable them to function optimally.
- **Unfair exclusion.** Shutting people out or preventing them having access to resources and information they are entitled to access. Preventing them having communication with other people.
- **Sexual harassment.** Objectifying men or women or treating them as sex objects. Joking about sex, gender or sexuality. Laughing along when others do. Using offensive sexualised language and trying and have sexual relationships with people you manage. Treat people with respect, no matter what their gender or sexual orientation.
- **Racial harassment.** Using or allowing racist language, such as making racist comments or jokes. Making stereotypical comments that demean people's race, culture or religion. Treat people with respect, regardless of their race, culture or religion.

This covers most of the common behaviours that are considered workplace bullying or harassment. Even if a manager is a Type A personality or has a strong management style, they do not have the right to bully people. Be a firm manager, of course! But also, be a fair one. Command respect rather than demand it.

Step 3: Call out unreasonable and destructive behaviour

When managers witness acts of bullying or harassment, they need to call it out. If they don't, their silence will be interpreted as condoning the behaviour.

There are several ways to do this, ranging from a gentle reminder to a clear reprimand. One simple and often successful way of calling out behaviour is simply to name it:

> "That's a put-down."
>
> "I notice you are yelling."
>
> "You are undermining him."

When this reflective technique is used, it brings attention to the behaviour without necessarily judging it. Sometimes naming it out loud is enough on its own to stop the behaviour. If people know you will call them out and that you will challenge their behaviour, they will get a consistent message, and that is important.

Another technique that is often used is to make an appeal to a standard:

> "Stop it. That's not OK."
>
> "That is inappropriate."

This technique is commonly used to prevent bullying or harassment. It calls attention to a standard or code of conduct. It is a useful tool, but it can backfire when someone says:

> "I don't think it's inappropriate?"

In some work groups many forms of incivility and low-level bullying become acceptable because people get used to these forms of behaviour. People tend to gravitate to the lowest form of civility when it is regularly displayed around them. Telling someone in this environment that the behaviour is inappropriate will not have much effect.

It may be useful to conduct an exercise where the team talks about behaviour they think is appropriate and what they think is inappropriate. Or it may be sufficient for the manager to make clear and regular statements about what is appropriate behaviour. This provides a standard that can be referred to and helps avoids arguments about what is or is not acceptable.

> "We have a policy about preventing bullying and harassment, and I want you to understand what bullying and harassment look like, so we can all make sure this doesn't happen. I have observed some of these behaviours here at times and I have been guilty of some of them myself. I have a responsibility to make sure that I don't bully and harass anyone, and I also have responsibility to stop it happening in our team. I hope you will join me in this goal for everyone's benefit. Let's get clear about what is and isn't bullying and harassment."

Starting a discussion about what is and isn't bullying and harassment is a very useful discussion to have, because it gets people thinking about behaviour and the effect of behaviour. It also gets people thinking about the types of behaviour that are respectful and reasonable. What is reasonable and what is unreasonable? What is appropriate and what is not inappropriate?

Another way of calling out behaviour is to appeal to impact. By describing the effect of a behaviour, it appeals to the person's sense of empathy:

> "That is threatening."
>
> "That's demeaning and offensive."

Sometimes this can be used in a more personal way:

> "I feel annoyed at the way you criticised one person in front of everyone else when that was unnecessary. Were you intending to publicly humiliate them?"
>
> "That may seem funny to you, but some people might find it offensive."
>
> "When you start getting loud, you shut people down."

Managers need to know how to call out behaviour because that is what managing behaviour is all about. They need to manage behaviour, because behaviour sometimes affects people negatively. Talk about behaviour, cause and effect.

In one organisation, the CEO heard rumours that another first-line manager was bullying her staff. The CEO organised some training on workplace bullying. At the beginning of each session, the CEO introduced the trainer and made these comments:

> "This is a subject that I personally feel strongly about. I hate bullying and I hate harassment. I realise that we can all sometimes say or do things that are offensive or hurtful to others. We should all be accountable for our behaviour, and I want you to know that if I do or say anything that intimidates, offends, or hurts you, then I want you to challenge me. I will listen and take your challenge on board, even if I may disagree with it. I will be accountable to you. I will do the same with you and I will challenge your behaviour if it is unreasonable and destructive.
>
> I also want you to know that if you experience bullying or harassment by anyone here, and you are unsure what to do about it, my door is open, and I will welcome you. Let's all work together to make this a great place to be."

The CEO set the scene and the trainer then commenced the session. In the next 2 weeks the CEO was approached by people who had been too afraid to speak up previously. The training sessions had opened the floodgates, and an investigation process began that exposed the bullying dynamics. The perpetrator was held to account and her regime of tyrannical behaviour toppled.

Change happens when people take a stand and call out inappropriate behaviour.

Chapter 2

Ways of Thinking about Bullying and Harassment

¶2-010 Workplace bullying

Workplace bullying is an issue that deserves considerable attention, analysis and understanding. Significant research undertaken in New Zealand and Australia indicates that bullying and harassment affect many workers and workplaces. It is a common hazard that damages people, sometimes severely, and employers have a legal duty of care to protect employees from harm.

Protecting people from bullying and harassment is not necessarily a simple thing to do. It is not a matter of creating a zero-tolerance policy, as this places the onus on vulnerable people to speak up and report bullying. This simplistic approach does not work well. Instead of zero tolerance, we need to focus on prevention. This means stopping bullying behaviour and creating a culture where people don't want to bully and are not rewarded for it. They manage their own behaviour and relationships because it is important to them and because they genuinely care about their effects on people they work with.

¶2-020 Historical perspectives on bullying

Bullying happens throughout our society, from the top structures to the bottom. It occurs within the realms of the rich and the poor, the advantaged and the disadvantaged. We see it in governments and in schools, families, societal groups and workplaces.

Bullying can be physical, but it is predominantly psychological. It is a form of psychological violence. It affects people's thinking, feelings and sense of self. As one adult said:

> "After being bullied as an adult, my life changed, and I have never fully recovered."

Bullying is associated with abuse of power and control. It can also be associated with cruelty. Bullies may be seen as cruel power players who seem to enjoy tormenting others. This aspect is deeply disturbing.

Another aspect of bullying is its link to weakness and cowardliness. Stories abound of people who have "stood up to a bully" and found that the bully has backed down. We may think of bullies as cowards who pick on those below them or who only choose to target those who have less resources or agency to fight back. Bullies "never pick on people their own size" is a widely held belief.

Fighting back against bullies is a popular notion internationally. It is easy to go down the story line that bullies are monsters that need to be defeated by fearless heroes. We have people calling themselves "bully-busters" and this promotes the idea that "bullying back" is the answer to bullying or that violence is the answer to violence.

These perspectives get us thinking about bullying in a certain way, but they also limit us and may even trap us.

¶2-030 Subjective experiences

People often define bullying subjectively. A common expression is:

> "I feel bullied."

People may say this after they have experienced an encounter they don't like. However, there is an assumption that if someone feels bullied, they must have been bullied. This may not be accurate. It is a personal perception. Don't assume it is true.

What does it mean when someone says that they feel bullied? Bullying is not a feeling. There is no emotion we can describe as, "bullied". Rather than being a feeling, it is an assessment or an interpretation of a situation. The person might feel hurt, anxious or afraid, but they attach a meaning to that feeling and conclude that they have been bullied. How do they make that assessment? On what criteria? It can be very subjective and unreliable.

It is not uncommon for the term bullying to be used indiscriminately and inappropriately. People have complained of being bullied in response to reasonable requests to do their jobs. They claim bullying when facing legitimate investigations or disciplinary processes. People have complained of bullying when they are in conflict or when they have been offended by not getting their way. The word gets used indiscriminately. This obscures the reality of genuine bullying.

It also creates problems for managers and supervisors, who have a responsibility to deal with such matters. Bullying is something more than a little pressure or a personal clash. Unfortunately, these subjective claims lead some managers to refuse to take the issue seriously. What is needed, though, is a more robust definition of bullying that has some level of objectivity. This is a challenge for legislators and policy writers, but it is necessary to distinguish bullying from other unpleasant interpersonal encounters.

Managers need to understand what is and what isn't bullying. They need to know where the line is between bullying and something else such as incivility or unfriendliness. This is not about making everyone friendly. That is impossible. The objective is not to make workplaces nice places to work, but to make them safe places to work.

People in workplaces also need to understand where the "line" is, so that they know what is acceptable or unacceptable. When that line is well understood, it can be reinforced and becomes a powerful force that shapes social and workplace interactions.

So how might we think about bullying?

There are 3 common paradigms or ways of thinking that people have in relation to workplace bullying and the way to approach it. They all have some value, and it is useful to be familiar with these different ways of thinking.

¶2-040 The behavioural paradigm

This view describes bullying as a form of behaviour. Bullying involves some type of action (or inaction) by someone (or a group) toward someone else (or another group). The behavioural paradigm breaks bullying down into sub-categories of behaviour. Bullying might involve shouting at someone or standing over someone. Bullying might also include the use of demeaning language toward a person, pranks or public humiliation. It might also involve undermining someone's work by secretly sabotaging them. Each of these forms of behaviour can be described as bullying behaviour.

By reducing the term bullying into different behavioural sub-categories, we can identify bullying in a clearer way. It is no longer a "feeling" but a form of behaviour. In a workplace we can identify and name specific types of behaviour. We can then create expectations that people should not accept those kinds of behaviour.

This is quite a useful paradigm for identifying bullying and managing people's behaviour. However, it does have some flaws:

Firstly, the behavioural paradigm assumes that, by explaining bullying as a form of behaviour, people will understand this and be able to adjust their behaviour accordingly. However, we are not computers that can be programmed, and some people may still use bullying behaviour despite having had training. Our behaviour is learned over many years and becomes a part of a pattern of other behaviours. Our behaviour is embedded in belief structures, and it can take considerable effort to change a single type of behaviour.

For example, despite knowing that displays of aggression and shouting are forms of bullying, Robert still does it when he becomes upset about an issue. When confronted afterwards, he apologises, but after a while he does it again. Robert learned to behave this way when he was 4 years old, and he is now 32.

What will it take for Robert to change his behaviour? These things are complex.

Secondly, people do not perceive their own behaviour the way others perceive it. Bullying and harassment involve perceptions, and we cannot assume that everyone sees or experiences things the same way.

"I was making a point."

"You were yelling and standing over me."

Thirdly, there is an inherent assumption with the behavioural paradigm that people choose their behaviour consciously and therefore they should be able to choose not to behave a certain way. This idea is simplistic. People often act habitually without thinking about how their behaviour might be perceived or experienced by someone else.

"That's just the way I am."

Obviously more is needed to prevent bullying than just describing a list of behaviours to be avoided. The behavioural paradigm is useful but has some limitations.

¶2-050 The pathological paradigm

This approach treats bullying as if it were a sickness or pathology of some kind. It changes the focus from "bullying" to whether someone is "a bully". It shifts from what a person does to what a person is. It assumes that there are some people in society who are "bullies" and that there are other people who are not bullies. It wrongly assumes that only some people bully others and that these people are pathological monsters of some sort.

Anyone can bully. If you use bullying behaviour in a situation, then you are being a bully in that situation. People can even bully themselves. They can abuse themselves, harm themselves, and be overly self-critical and self-destructive. We bully when we use bullying behaviour. Some do it worse than others, but anyone can do it.

In workplaces where the pathological paradigm is dominant, this leads to a culture where people are quick to label others and characterise them as bullies. It also leads to people defending themselves against accusations of being a bully:

"I am not a bully. How dare you say that!"

The heat rises, and there is usually an increased level of complaint-making, investigations, and calls for disciplinary action. Anyone accused of bullying is given an unpleasant label that sticks to them. The increased level of adversarial dynamics generally raises the level of toxicity in the work environment, and bullying may increase on all levels.

People who hold to this pathological paradigm often feel entitled to "name and shame" others loudly and recklessly. They are quick to "point the finger" and "go to war", because if someone is a bully there is nothing else to do about it than attack them. They are monsters, and monsters need to be eliminated. Sadly, these self-righteous crusaders are often blind to their own destructive behaviour, making false and inaccurate allegations, defaming, undermining and fomenting hostility. These are often the worst kinds of bullies.

However, there is some truth to the pathological paradigm. There are some people who do bully more and to a worse degree than others. Dr Robert Hare, a Canadian expert on psychopathy, estimates that 1% of the population have this personality disorder. However, if bullying affects 20% of workers (as estimated by WorkSafe New Zealand), then it is unlikely that all bullying is done by less than 1% of the population. So who does the rest of the bullying? It is the rest of the population who do not have a personality disorder. These are people who sometimes behave badly, who lack insight, self-awareness and empathy, and who feel a sense of entitlement to act in a hostile manner toward others at times, especially when they get into conflict, feel threatened, or are offended by something.

Some people bully without thinking that what they are doing is bullying. Some people have blind spots and don't understand how their behaviour affects others, or if they do they don't really care much about it. This is by far the most common type of bullying in organisations.

This kind of bullying is called "accidental bullying" by some writers. This is not a great way of describing bullying, but people sometimes act badly, especially when they feel upset. Does this make them monsters? No. Therefore, we need to step back from characterising people in this way and understand that bullying is not a sickness or a personality type; it is a form of behaviour. Let's focus on preventing bullying, rather than labelling people as bullies.

¶2-060 The cultural paradigm

The cultural paradigm views bullying and harassment as things that exist within a social system. The social system, with its beliefs, norms, structures, processes and practices, allows bullying and harassment to occur, not necessarily by an overt declaration but instead by minimising, normalising and allowing bullying and harassment to happen as if they were inevitable and normal ways of behaving.

In cultures where bullying and harassment thrive, there is usually a high degree of acceptance of bullying and harassing behaviour. People will often say:

> "That's just the way things are here," or "That's just the way he/she is."

The behaviour will be downplayed by language. Instead of calling it bullying, people will call it robust or strong behaviour. Instead of calling it sexual harassment, they will call it banter or fun.

Gaslighting is found in workplace cultures where bullying and harassment thrive. Gaslighting is a form of manipulation that makes people question and doubt their own experiences:

> "I am being bullied."
>
> "I think you are too sensitive."

In workplace cultures where bullying and harassment thrive, there will be a lack of training or discussion about bullying and harassment as a health and safety issue. These issues will not be talked about openly. Allegations will seldom be investigated thoroughly, and instead the perpetrators will be protected and supported.

This is known as a toxic culture. It breeds toxic behaviour.

Targets of bullying and harassment will often be seen as weak, overly sensitive, problematic people. Sometimes they will be labelled as troublemakers or even worse as "dobbers" or traitors within the organisation.

Speaking up about bullying would be a quick way to exit oneself from such an organisation, so it is unlikely that people will speak up at all within this kind of culture.

> "We don't have a problem with bullying here. We don't get any complaints."

When bullying or harassment occurs at the top level of an organisation, the perpetrators will often be protected and supported at all costs. The organisation may engage in resilience training programmes to help staff endure the destructive dynamics. However, the perpetrators are never held to account, and they are unlikely to change.

In this type of culture bad behaviour is often described as good, and good behaviour may be seen as bad. The truth is fake and what's fake becomes the truth. It is a topsy-turvy, upside-down world that protects perpetrators from accountability. Managers and staff at lower levels in the organisation will often mimic the bullying and harassing behaviours modelled by those at the top. In this way the whole organisation becomes a toxic mess that perpetuates a culture of collusion. All of this ensures a generational cycle of abuse that continues to infect the future.

It is impossible to stop bullying and harassment when the culture supports this behaviour. Unless those in power take steps to change the culture, it will never be a safe or secure place to work.

The cultural paradigm reminds us that things always happen in a context and within a culture. By changing the culture, we can therefore change things that happen within it.

> "Bullying happens because people allow it to happen."

¶2-070 Sexual harassment and misogyny

The prevalence of sexual harassment in workplaces does not appear to have diminished much after about 30 years of research, new policies and training programmes. The "Me Too" movement is a testimony to the failure of these measures. Why is this pernicious behavioural hazard so difficult to eliminate?

As any gardener knows, weeds keep growing even though you have cut them back on the surface. The problem with most sexual harassment is that there is a root system that keeps the behavioural weed popping up again and again. That main root system is misogyny, and this is seldom addressed sufficiently in workplaces.

Misogyny is a belief system that is deeply embedded in our western cultural history. It has often been described as the hatred of women. A better description of misogyny is that it is the fear of women having power.

Misogyny is about power, and sexual harassment is a phenomenon associated with power. Most commonly it is about male dominance and privilege. Those who are deeply entrenched in misogyny use sexual harassment to dominate women and keep them in gender-based, stereotypical roles. They typically do not change unless they address their misogynistic beliefs and patterns of behaviour.

Historically women have been positioned by men into lesser roles than men. Just over 100 years ago women had no right to vote. They were not seen as being equal to men and were expected to follow different social norms than men. Fortunately, in the last 60 years or so, society has advanced the view that women should have equality with men, but this at odds with misogyny. Misogyny says women should be subservient to men, that they should be relegated to a lesser place because they are less capable, a place that men decide because men are entitled to make such decisions simply because they are male. The sad thing is that it is not just men who support misogyny. It is so deeply rooted in our societal and cultural traditions that it is simply regarded as normal.

Traditionally, men have been valued for their power, money and sexual prowess. Women, in contrast, have traditionally been valued for their attractiveness (to men), their home-making abilities, and their ability to bear and nurture children.

This social system has been the norm for men and women throughout the centuries. Men have been the "Kings of the Castle", and women have been the homemakers. In terms of the dynamics of power, men have been at the top and women have been at the bottom. Traditionally, men have employed forms of violence and bullying in families to maintain their dominance. Women have learned to become demure and subservient. Domestic violence is a system of power and control, and sexual dominance is a part of it.

The James Bond archetype is typical example of a misogynist. In every James Bond movie, James generally relates to women as sexual objects to be conquered, but he also relates to his superior "M" as a mythical mother figure. She tuts over his sexual dalliances. James just can't help himself and is never really expected to. After all, he is "just a man".

The typical modern-day sexual harasser is a man who acts something like James Bond. He either treats women as sexual objects or relates to them as mother figures. He somehow believes he is not offensive. He thinks his comments, jokes and sexual innuendoes are a way of telling a woman that she is highly valued. They are really compliments that she should appreciate and are not to be seen as offensive.

The male sexual harasser may be clever, witty, charming and respectful in some ways, but he also has an over-developed sense of sexual entitlement. He is a master of flattery and sees himself as an admirer of female beauty, not a hater of women. He just cannot help himself make comments about women's bodies and his own sexual interest in them because, after all, he is "just a man". When women laugh along with his cheekiness, he is rewarded, and his misogynistic behaviour is reinforced.

Here is a sad story of a male sexual harasser of women:

> Matt is a manager of a sales team. He has two young women in his team, and although he is at least 20 years older than them, and married, he sees nothing wrong in sexually harassing them. He would never describe his behaviour as harassment. He thinks he is just being friendly and funny.
>
> His methods follow a typical grooming process. It starts with comments about their attractive hair styles or dress sense, and he will also use sexual innuendo and jokes. Matt's behaviour gets laughs from the men and from some older women, who respond with sexual banter in return. The two young women find themselves unsure of Matt. He is quite kind and friendly, but they feel increasingly uncomfortable. As time goes on, they realise that everyone seems to accept Matt's behaviour, but the two women feel more and more distrusting and isolated.
>
> Matt progresses his grooming to the point where he sometimes talks about his sexual activities and his sexual desires with the two women. He calls them girls not women. He asks questions about their sexual interests and what they "got up to" on the weekend. He laughs and can be friendly, but the women have come to see him as creepy. He makes specific comments about their bodies. On two occasions he has physically touched them. The hand around the shoulder. The full body hugs. It is all very subtle, and Matt is a master game player.
>
> People at work generally like Matt. He gets laughs. The two women display frowns or make comments such as, "Yuk", but Matt laughs it off.

> The two women approach a senior manager, and the manager asks them to make a complaint. Matt is put off work as the investigation process commences. While off work, Matt phones his male workmates and tells them these women are trying to "stitch him up" and "bring him down" by accusing him of the most terrible acts of sexual harassment. He paints himself as the victim and the two women as vengeful man-haters. The women become the target of gossip at work, and some men now avoid them. They have walked out of the room when the women have entered. The women are treated like outcasts.
>
> The investigation finds some evidence of sexual harassment, and Matt is given a warning. When he returns from his suspension, he mostly ignores the women and is very official in his tone when he is required to communicate with them. After two days, both women resign, significantly stressed and disillusioned.
>
> Matt continues to work in this organisation. Senior management admit they have been too lenient on sexual banter, and it is regrettable that the women have resigned. However, Matt stays on and the workplace culture continues.

Matt probably won't change, despite having a warning. He may tone things down a bit for a while, but unless he gets some focused therapy that gets to the root beliefs he has about women, he will keep treating women in this way. To him, it is normal and the way men behave around women. Matt is unlikely to change, because the social system supports his misogyny. Unless there is leadership from the top, this dynamic will continue.

Not all sexual harassment is based on misogyny. Some sexual harassment is based on homophobia and gender identity. However, a significant amount of sexual harassment by men against women is based on misogyny. Unless we begin to address the root system, we will continue to produce the same weed.

¶2-080 Racial harassment and hate

Some people hate what they are afraid of or what looks different or foreign to them. They hate what they don't understand. Most racial harassment involves hate. While we focus on unconscious bias, discrimination, prejudice or bigotry, the deeper issue is that of hate.

Hate is associated with 2 other emotions: anger and fear.

> In a workplace, sudden growth triggered a recruitment drive. In six months, staff numbers almost doubled and most of the new people were of a different race and ethnicity. Tensions within the group increased and the company did little to assist the development of relationships.
>
> Racist slogans began to appear on toilet walls. Racist name calling, intimidation and threats became a norm and there were two occasions of

physical violence. People refused to work with each other, and factions developed that affected production.

An external facilitator was employed to resolve racial harassment in the team. Management expected the facilitator to provide training sessions on racial harassment, but the facilitator had different ideas. He talked to each faction separately to try to understand what was happening and how people were being affected.

The facilitator discovered that, although there was hatred, there was also fear and ignorance. He asked each faction to elect a representative to be part of a change leadership group. Each faction chose their most ardent warrior, because they were afraid of losing ground. The facilitator expected this and welcomed it, seeing the possibility of emerging leadership roles. He then worked with the change leadership group and began by creating an opportunity for each person to speak openly and honestly within a set of agreed guidelines.

After one session, the change leadership group united with a common purpose and goals. They identified misconceptions, misunderstandings, and barriers to working together. They addressed what they were afraid of and what they wanted and didn't want. The "warriors" then worked with their own teams and focused on reconciliation and building common understandings.

The warriors had become peacemakers. The factions were brought together, and they developed new ways of working together, operating on the development of mutuality, trust and cohesion. They got to know each other as people. This created a shift in the culture.

¶2-090 Mobbing

Most of the original bullying research in Scandinavian countries in the 1980s and 1990s focused on the issue of mobbing. Mobbing is group bullying. An example of this occurred within the trades industry. The apprentice was bullied by the tradesmen. The tradesmen were bullied themselves when they were apprentices. There was no single bully, but several people became involved at various levels.

Within the trades, this kind of bullying was not previously considered bullying: "It is just boys being boys." However, when an apprentice in Queensland was bound with masking tape, put in a drum, and sprinkled with lighter fluid, then set alight, the authorities were alerted, and the organisation was fined a significant amount for their breach of health and safety laws.

The young male apprentice was the target of significant mobbing, which included being verbally abused, threatened, teased and physically assaulted on a weekly basis. This went on for months under the eyes of everyone, who turned away and did nothing.

In New Zealand, it has been common for people to experience mobbing after making a complaint of being bullied. The general trend is that it starts with bullying by one person and turns into mobbing after the target has spoken up.

The 0800 ZEROBULLY helpline in New Zealand found that 51% of callers who initially experienced bullying went on to experience mobbing as well. The mobbing occurred after they had made a complaint. Most ended up leaving their workplaces. Some took personal grievances but often found the process mostly unfair. The most common financial payout was under $5,000 and was settled in mediation with a gagging order to protect the employer from being publicly criticised. Some might consider $5,000 a large sum. However, when lawyers need to be paid and the target is left without a job, it is a paltry amount. It does little to compensate for the significant stress, health impacts and ongoing financial impact due to unemployment.

It is no wonder that many targets see themselves as being disadvantaged not only by their workplaces but also by the external government agencies that have been set up to address workplace grievances.

Chapter 3

Legal Frameworks and Provisions

¶3-010 Australia and New Zealand legal frameworks

Australia and New Zealand have many similarities and some differences in legal frameworks when it comes to workplace bullying and harassment. The following is a brief description of each country's legal frameworks and provisions.

¶3-020 Australia: Fair Work Act 2009 (Cth)

The Fair Work Act 2009 (Cth) is one of the primary pieces of legislation applying to employment in most of Australia's workplaces. It provides the minimum standards and regulations for employment in the national workplace arena. The Act makes provision for addressing workplace bullying and sexual harassment.

The Fair Work Act 2009 (Cth) defines bullying in s 789FD(1), and the Fair Work Commission refers to this definition in its Anti-Bullying Benchbook:

> "Workplace bullying occurs when an individual or a group of individuals repeatedly behaves unreasonably towards a worker, or a group of workers at work and the behaviour creates a risk to health and safety."[1]

This is very similar to the definition used in both Australian and New Zealand health and safety legislation.

The important elements are clearly laid out in this definition. To constitute bullying, the behaviour must be:

- repeated
- unreasonable, and
- create a risk to health and safety.

This means that bullying cannot be a single act. There must be some repetition over time. It could be repetition within a range of bullying behaviour that would include (but is not limited to) behaviour that is victimising, humiliating, intimidating, or threatening.

What sort of behaviour is considered within the range?

- aggressive and intimidating conduct

1 *Anti-Bullying Benchbook*, Fair Work Commission, Commonwealth of Australia (2019), p15.

- belittling or humiliating comments
- victimisation
- spreading malicious rumours
- practical jokes or initiation
- exclusion from work-related events, and
- unreasonable work expectations.[2]

The repeated behaviour also needs to be unreasonable. This is an important element.

> "Unreasonable behaviour is described as behaviour that a reasonable person, having regard to the circumstances, may see as unreasonable. In other words, it is an objective test."[3]

The repeated, unreasonable behaviour must also create a risk of harm to someone's health and safety. However, under anti-bullying laws, proof of actual harm does not have to be established as a fact, provided that a risk to health and safety created by bullying behaviour is demonstrated.

A risk to health and safety means exposure to potential danger to health and safety and must be real and not conceptual[4] The repeated, unreasonable bullying behaviour that creates a risk of harm to a worker's health and safety must also be directed at a worker while at work in a "constitutionally-covered business".[5] "Reasonable management action conducted in a reasonable manner does not constitute workplace bullying."[6]

Section 789FD(2) of the Fair Work Act 2009 (Cth) is not so much an "exclusion" but a "qualification" on the definition of when a worker is bullied at work and is comprised of 3 elements:

- "the behaviour must be management action
- it must be reasonable for the management action to be taken, and
- the management action must be carried out in a manner that is reasonable".[7]

The Fair Work Act 2009 (Cth) applies to paid and voluntary workers but does not apply to Australian Defence Force officers or enlisted members.

Sexual harassment is defined under the Sex Discrimination Act 1984:

> A person sexually harasses another person if they:

2 *Anti-Bullying Benchbook,* Fair Work Commission, Commonwealth of Australia (2019), p 16.

3 *Anti-Bullying Benchbook,* Fair Work Commission, Commonwealth of Australia (2019), p 41.

4 *Anti-Bullying Benchbook,* Fair Work Commission, Commonwealth of Australia (2019), p 41.

5 Fair Work Act 2009 (Cth), s 789FD(1).

6 Fair Work Act, s 789FD(2). *Sexual Harassment Benchbook,* Fair Work Commission, Commonwealth of Australia (2019), p 54.

7 *Anti-Bullying Benchbook,* Fair Work Commission, Commonwealth of Australia (2019), p 61.

- make an unwelcome sexual advance, or an unwelcome request for sexual favours to the person harassed, or
- engage in other unwelcome conduct of a sexual nature to the person harassed.

For a person to have sexually harassed someone, it has to be reasonable to expect that in the situation, there's a possibility that their behaviour would offend, humiliate, or intimidate the harassed person.[8]

¶3-030 The Fair Work Commission

The Fair Work Commission (FWC) is Australia's national workplace or employment relations tribunal and has jurisdiction to resolve disputes and make anti-bullying orders or orders to stop sexual harassment at work.

For the FWC to make an order to stop bullying, it must be satisfied "not only that a worker has been bullied at work by an individual or a group of individuals, but **also** that there is a risk that the worker will continue to be bullied at work **by that** individual or group of individuals".[9]

When an application is made, the FWC informs the applicant's employer and the person who is alleged to have conducted the bullying. The Commission is required to consider the evidence and whether the evidence constitutes bullying behaviour. This is not a complete investigation of all allegations but an objective assessment.

If the application is accepted by the FWC, a conference or hearing will be organised so that the matter can be heard. The Commission may conduct mediation or conciliation, make a recommendation to the parties, or express an opinion. Conferences are held in private, but decisions are published. Hearings are more formal than conferences. They are conducted in public and result in a decision.

The FWC can make any order it considers appropriate other than ordering financial payments to be made. It can order:

- the specific individual or group of individuals to stop the specified bullying behaviour
- an employer to regularly monitor behaviours
- compliance with an employer's anti-bullying policy
- the provision of information and additional support and training to workers, and
- a review of the employer's workplace bullying policy.

8 Sex Discrimination Act 1984, s 28A.

9 *Anti-Bullying Benchbook*, Fair Work Commission, Commonwealth of Australia (2019), p 59.

The goal of orders is to prevent further bullying or sexual harassment, resolve matters, and enable working relationships to resume.

Orders may not be limited to the employer only but could also apply to other individuals or groups of individuals involved in the behaviour. Orders could be based on behaviour such as threats made outside of the workplace if such threats related to work.[10]

A person who applies to the FWC for an order to stop bullying can also seek the intervention of a workplace health and safety regulator. These regulators may:

- send investigators to workplaces to investigate incidents
- issue prohibition or improvement notices
- seek enforceable undertakings
- commence prosecutions under work, health and safety legislation.[11]

Failure to comply with an order set by the FWC is a criminal offence and the matter can be referred to the Federal Court of Australia, the Federal Circuit and Family Court of Australia or a state or territory court. These are civil remedy proceedings, and the Court may impose pecuniary penalties or other orders.

¶3-040 New Zealand: Employment Relations Act 2000

The Employment Relations Act 2000 is New Zealand's primary legislation for employment and provides a framework for managing employment relations. The Act addresses sexual and racial harassment; however, it does not specifically address workplace bullying and does not define what workplace bullying is.

The Act allows individuals to take a personal grievance claim if they believe they have been treated unfairly or unreasonably by their employer. Personal grievances must be lodged within 90 days of an incident, and the main grounds for a personal grievance are:

- unjustified dismissal
- unjustified disadvantage
- sexual harassment
- racial harassment
- discrimination.

Sexual harassment is defined in the Employment Relations Act:

10 *Anti-Bullying Benchbook,* Fair Work Commission, Commonwealth of Australia (2019), p 115.

11 *Anti-Bullying Benchbook,* Fair Work Commission, Commonwealth of Australia (2019), p 118.

> For the purposes of sections 103(1)(d) and 123(d), an employee is sexually harassed in that employee's employment if that employee's employer or a representative of that employer—
>
> **(a)** directly or indirectly makes a request of that employee for sexual intercourse, sexual contact, or other form of sexual activity that contains—
>
> **(i)** an implied or overt promise of preferential treatment in that employee's employment; or
>
> **(ii)** an implied or overt threat of detrimental treatment in that employee's employment; or
>
> **(iii)** an implied or overt threat about the present or future employment status of that employee; or
>
> **(b)** by—
>
> **(i)** the use of language (whether written or spoken) of a sexual nature; or
>
> **(ii)** the use of visual material of a sexual nature; or
>
> **(iii)** physical behaviour of a sexual nature,—
>
> directly or indirectly subjects the employee to behaviour that is unwelcome or offensive to that employee (whether or not that is conveyed to the employer or representative) and that, either by its nature or through repetition, has a detrimental effect on that employee's employment, job performance, or job satisfaction.[12]

Racial harassment is defined in the Employment Relations Act:

> For the purposes of sections 103(1)(e) and 123(d), an employee is racially harassed in the employee's employment if the employee's employer or a representative of that employer uses language (whether written or spoken), or visual material, or physical behaviour that directly or indirectly—
>
> **(a)** expresses hostility against, or brings into contempt or ridicule, the employee on the ground of the race, colour, or ethnic or national origins of the employee; and
>
> **(b)** is hurtful or offensive to the employee (whether or not that is conveyed to the employer or representative); and
>
> **(c)** has, either by its nature or through repetition, a detrimental effect on the employee's employment, job performance, or job satisfaction.[13]

12 Employment Relations Act 2000, s 108.

13 Employment Relations Act 2000, s 109.

Although workplace bullying is not mentioned in the Act, a person who is bullied should be able to make a claim of unjustified disadvantage if they have been bullied or make a claim of unjustified dismissal if they have been unfairly dismissed or had to leave a workplace because it became untenable for them to continue. The last mentioned is often referred to as constructive dismissal. It could follow bullying by the employer or a situation in which an employer fails to address bullying by a colleague of the employee.

While these avenues may be available to those who have been bullied, the Act does not specifically address the issue of workplace bullying. The 90-day limit may also be problematic in cases of bullying where repeated bullying has occurred over longer periods of time.

¶3-050 The Mediation Service and Employment Relations Authority

The Employment Relations Act also establishes statutory bodies that have exclusive powers over employment matters. The 3 main institutions are:

- the Mediation Service (operating under the Ministry of Business, Innovation and Employment (MBIE))
- the Employment Relations Authority (ERA)
- the Employment Court.

Mediation is the preferred and generally mandated initial problem-solving tool between the parties. If employment is ongoing, a settlement between the employer and the employee can have the advantage of addressing future conduct either by the bully, or by the employer in respect of the bully, or bullying conduct in the workplace generally.

If the matter cannot be resolved by mediation, then it can be examined by the Employment Relations Authority. Challenges to determinations of the Authority can be made to the Employment Court. Unlike the Mediation Service, the Employment Relations Authority and the Employment Court can grant remedies to a wronged party. These can include reinstatement if a person has been dismissed, reimbursement of lost wages, compensation (damages), and costs.

¶3-060 Australian Work health and safety legislation

Work health and safety (WHS) legislation falls mainly within the jurisdiction of the Australian state and territory governments. The exception to this is workers who are covered by Commonwealth WHS legislation. Most states and territories have adopted the Work Health and Safety Act 2011 as a model; however, Victoria has not done so, although the statutory and regulatory schemes in that state is similar in terms of workplace bullying concepts.

These concepts include:

- All workers must comply with health and safety requirements in their workplaces.
- All workers are required to take reasonable care that their acts or omissions do not adversely affect other workers.
- Officers or people in control of businesses or undertakings (PCBUs) have an obligation to ensure, as far as reasonably practicable, the health and safety of their workers while they are at work. They can be personally liable if there is a failure to meet WHS obligations.
- The definition of "health" includes psychological health.

If a worker is injured at work, including an injury caused by bullying, that person can make a complaint to their WHS regulatory body. Once a complaint is received, the regulator can investigate. If a breach is found, the regulator can enforce compliance notices or prosecute both organisations and individuals.

Those who are injured (physically or psychologically) at work can be compensated, whether or not the employer has been found to be responsible for the injury. The Australian workers' compensation framework operates in parallel to its WHS laws. Although Australian compensation laws provide for physical and psychological injuries, workers can find it difficult to satisfy their employer's compensation insurer, and while the worker can challenge a finding by approaching the relevant court, this can be a difficult and arduous course of action for a worker who has already suffered psychological injury.[14]

The following definition is used by Safe Work Australia:

> "Workplace bullying is repeated and unreasonable behaviour directed towards a worker or a group of workers that creates a risk to health and safety"[15]

This definition is aligned with the Fair Work Act 2009 (Cth) and contains the three main elements of its definition, namely that the bullying behaviour needs to be:

- repeated
- unreasonable, and
- create a risk to health and safety.

---

14 J. Catanzariti and K. Egan, *Workplace Bullying*, 2nd edition, LexisNexis (2021), p 15.

15 "Guide for Preventing and Responding to Workplace Bullying", Safe Work Australia (2016), p 5.

¶3-070 New Zealand workplace health and safety legislation

WorkSafe New Zealand is the primary health and safety regulator administering the Health and Safety at Work Act 2015. In its guidelines on "Preventing and Responding to Bullying at Work", the following definition is provided:

> "Workplace bullying is repeated and unreasonable behaviour directed towards a worker or a group of workers that can lead to physical or psychological harm.
>
> - Repeated behaviour is persistent (occurs more than once) and can involve a range of actions over time.
> - Unreasonable behaviour means actions that a reasonable person in the same circumstances would see as unreasonable. It includes victimising, humiliating, intimidating or threatening a person.
> - Bullying may also include harassment, discrimination or violence . . ."[16]

WorkSafe acknowledges Safe Work Australia for the use of its content in their guide.

There are obvious similarities in the definitions used in both Australia and New Zealand, although one small difference is where WorkSafe New Zealand has modified the "risk to health and safety" to "can lead to physical and psychological harm".

WorkSafe New Zealand has powers to investigate complaints of bullying, but there are no specific guidelines relating to its role in investigating, or bringing prosecutions for, bullying or harassment. At the date of writing this book, there have been no prosecutions by WorkSafe for workplace bullying.

¶3-080 Australia and New Zealand common law

Under common law, employers owe their employees a duty of care. This duty of care involves taking reasonable care for their employees' safety or, of particular relevance in the context of workplace bullying, taking reasonable care to avoid the risk that an employee will suffer harm as a result of their employment. If harm is reasonably foreseeable, and an employer fails to act, this could result in a claim of negligence or breach of the implied contractual duty to provide and maintain a safe workplace. Damages for such a failure could ensue (New Zealand health and safety legislation is primarily based around fines for offences committed under that legislation).

16 "Preventing and Responding to Bullying at Work", WorkSafe NZ (2017), p 8.

Australia and New Zealand criminal offences

In some cases, serious instances of bullying can constitute criminal offences. An example of this is when criminal assault or sexual assault has occurred.

In Australia, the Victorian State Government enacted "Brodie's Law" after the death of Brodie Panlock in 2006. Brodie, a 19-year-old café worker, was bullied by her co-workers to the extent that she committed suicide. The perpetrators of the bullying could not be charged with a serious criminal offence under the Crimes Act 1958 (Crimes Act), but they were convicted and fined under the provisions of the Occupational Health and Safety Act 2004. Brodie's Law amended the Crimes Act to expand the list of 'stalking' behaviours to include:[17]

- making threats to the victim
- using abusive or offensive words to, or in the presence of, the victim
- performing abusive or offensive acts in the presence of the victim
- directing abusive or offensive acts toward the victim, or
- acting in any other way that could reasonably be expected to cause a victim to engage in self-harm.

Brodie's Law also amended the Personal Safety Intervention Orders Act 2010 (in Victoria) to allow a person to obtain certain orders against a perpetrator.

These legal amendments are not Australia-wide but only applicable in the state of Victoria.

In New Zealand, the Harassment Act 1997 (HA), makes harassment and stalking a criminal offence in certain circumstances. It is designed to protect people who experience, at least twice over a 12-month period, behaviour described as watching, loitering, following, accosting, interfering with another person's property, or acting in ways that cause the person to fear for their safety ("safety" including mental well-being). People who are being harassed may apply for restraining orders against the person harassing them.

¶3-090 Human rights legislation in Australia and New Zealand

In Australia, human rights are recognised and protected at the Federal, state, and tertiary levels. The Australian Human Rights Commission Act 1986 (AHRCA) details the powers and functions of the Australian Human Rights Commission (the Commission) as the Commonwealth agency responsible for monitoring and promoting human rights protection. The Commission also has responsibilities under the Racial Discrimination Act1975, the Equal Opportunity Act 1984, the Disability Discrimination Act 1992, the Sex Discrimination Act 1984, and the Age Discrimination Act 2004.

17 Catanzariti and K. Egan, *Workplace Bullying*, 2nd Edition, LexisNexis (2021), pp 15–16.

If the Commission receives a complaint, it will initially seek to resolve the complaint by conciliation. If this fails, the complaint may be forwarded to the Federal Court of Australia or the Federal Circuit and Family Court of Australia.

The New Zealand Human Rights Act 1993 (HRA) focuses primarily on discrimination. Discrimination occurs where a person is treated unfairly or less favourably than another person in the same or similar circumstances. The Human Rights Commission can investigate cases of bullying if there has been discrimination on the specified grounds of sexual and racial harassment. It cannot investigate claims of bullying on their own.

The grounds of discrimination are limited to the following:

- sex
- marital status
- religious belief
- ethical belief
- colour, race, or ethnic or national origins
- disability
- age
- political opinion
- employment status
- family status
- sexual orientation.

The HRA covers sexual and racial harassment at work, at school, and in other areas.

The Human Rights Commission has the power to facilitate the resolution of disputes and can also investigate breaches of the Human Rights Act. The Human Rights Review Tribunal can impose penalties on organisations as well as individuals. A person who alleges discrimination has to choose which procedure to use: a personal grievance in the Employment Relations Authority or the complaints procedure for breach of the Human Rights Act.

¶3-100 Cyber-bullying legislation

The Australian Online Safety Act 2021 (OSA) made previously existing laws for online safety more expansive and stronger. It also made online service providers more accountable for the online safety of the people who use their services. Complaints of cyber bullying can be made to the eSafety Commissioner. Under the new laws, online service providers, social media companies and other websites are compelled to remove content deemed to be bullying within 24 hours of receiving a removal notice or face fines.

In New Zealand the Harmful Digital Communications Act 2015 (HDCA) seeks to deter, prevent, and mitigate harm caused by digital communications. Harm means serious emotional distress. This can include sending offensive or threatening emails, texts, or online messages, including spreading damaging rumours and publishing invasive or distressing photos and videos. Digital communication means any form of electronic communication, including websites, blogs, comments sections, social media sites and phone apps.

The HDCA aims to provide a quick, efficient, and relatively cheap legal avenue for people dealing with serious or repeated harmful digital communication.[18]

Complaints must first be made to NetSafe for investigation, and if the matter is not resolved a person may apply to the District Court. The Court has powers to order material to be taken down and to issue cease and desist orders, and anyone who ignores the District Court's orders can be prosecuted and penalised.

¶3-110 Comments

What should the role of an external agency be when it comes to matters of bullying and harassment? We need laws to define what is acceptable and unacceptable. If there are no legal consequences for people who bully and harass, or there are no consequences for organisations that allow bullying and harassment, it is unlikely that the problem will be addressed adequately.

However, if external agencies get involved whenever a problem arises, this will be overly disruptive and excessively burdensome for employers and the external agencies required to hear cases and make judgments. Unless external agencies can deliver interventions quickly, targets of bullying and harassment will also be affected negatively by having to wait for long periods of time to have their cases heard and resolved. Justice delayed will be experienced as justice denied. The stress caused by bullying and harassment may be significant, but the stress involved in fighting for justice through the courts may be even worse.

The onus is primarily on employers to create safe workplaces and to prevent bullying and harassment from occurring within their own organisations. When employees raise issues internally, they should be responded to promptly and effectively. Employers need to build their own internal capacity to address issues, but they need practical assistance and guidance from external agencies. Unless matters are addressed early, they will deteriorate, creating far more problems for employers. Once matters within a workplace move to formal complaint and investigation processes, the likelihood of significant disruption increases exponentially. It is common for people to leave their employment because of the impact on them of formal processes.

18 See netsafe.org.nz.

This means that employers need to build their internal capacity to resolve issues early. Informal processes that are restorative and remedial are vitally important because they can change the destructive dynamics. This is a significant challenge that employers face in the new century.

Australia's Fair Work Commission allows for quick and effective orders to stop bullying, and these orders can be made to the employer as well as the individuals named as alleged perpetrators. This intervention aims to prevent further bullying and carries the threat of criminal court action if bullying continues. This intervention may be effective in preventing future bullying. However, it does not address past incidents. It may help an employee remain in the workplace and resolve matters that are a threat to their employment. If a person leaves a workplace, the orders are of no consequence.

New Zealand's personal grievance process is the opposite. It focuses on addressing what has occurred in the recent past (a 90-day limit). Apart from the mediation process, it does not take any action to prevent bullying in the future. The Employment Relations Act does not define bullying as a specific phenomenon as it does sexual harassment. It focuses on the past and seeks to initially resolve issues through mediation, before allowing an applicant to seek damages through the Employment Relations Authority. This is a lengthy process that may take many months, and it brings the target of bullying into an adversarial dynamic with the employer. It does not address the perpetrators. The process is lengthy and can be ineffective for targets and many targets leave their employment because of this.

It is important to address the past and the future. Interventions that prevent further incidents and hold the employer and the perpetrator to account have obvious advantages by reducing the potential for further harm. However, it is vital that these interventions happen quickly to limit further damage. Past incidents that have damaged a target and may have caused them significant psychological, physical and financial harm should also be addressed.

Chapter 4

Elements of Bullying

¶4-010 Defining workplace bullying

It is important to have a clear definition of workplace bullying if we are to make progress in preventing it. Definitions allow us to distinguish one thing from another. The problem is that bullying is difficult to define accurately. How do we distinguish bullying from other forms of difficult behaviour, incivility or unfriendliness? Bullying is more than simply being unfriendly or irritable.

As discussed in the last chapter, there are some similarities in definitions of workplace bullying used by health and safety regulators in both Australia and New Zealand. Workplace bullying involves certain kinds of behaviour that are:

- repeated (within the range of bullying behaviour)
- unreasonable
- a risk to health and safety.

This definition focuses on certain elements of behaviour and the potential impact of the behaviour.

¶4-020 Intention and power

The health and safety definition is not the only definition used in employment or criminal court hearings. The New Zealand Employment Relations Authority has referred to another definition of bullying that includes the following elements:[1]

- repeated actions
- carried out with the desire to gain power or dominance
- carried out with the intention to cause fear and distress.

This definition does not focus on the nature of the behaviour or whether the behaviour is reasonable or not. Neither does it focus on the likely impact of the behaviour on those who are affected by it. Instead, this definition focuses on the intention and motivation of the perpetrator.

In addition, this definition creates further complexity and difficulty for investigators, because it requires them to assess intention and "power" in a relationship. What does "to gain power" mean exactly? This is open to

1 *Kneebone v Schizophrenia Fellowship Waikato Inc* ERA Auckland AA31/07, 13 February 2007.

speculation. These aspects are very difficult to determine and may unnecessarily complicate matters.

What if someone uses bullying behaviour and they claim they did not intend to bully or cause fear and distress? This is a common excuse used by perpetrators. What if there is a lack of evidence to prove that the perpetrator intended to cause fear or distress?

> "I tried to control the situation and I did use insults and was critical, but it wasn't my intention to cause fear and distress. I was focused on getting them to improve."

The intention to act in a particular way should not determine whether the behaviour is unreasonable or that it poses a risk of physical or psychological harm. Intention is a matter that could be assessed when it comes to the disciplinary process. For example, if someone uses bullying behaviour without knowing their behaviour is likely to cause harm, this is different from someone who uses bullying behaviour knowing it is likely to cause harm. Both have bullied. However, one is far more deliberate and may require a different response from the employer.

Intention needs to be established for a murder charge. When intention is not present the charge may be reduced to manslaughter. What then of bullying? There is not a manslaughter version of bullying.

¶4-030 Forms of bullying behaviour

Bullying behaviour is often described by the effect it has on people. For example, bullying may be described as intimidating, humiliating, undermining or victimising behaviour. It is common for people to describe bullying behaviour this way. The problem is that it is very subjective. What is threatening to you may not be threatening to me.

Therefore, it is important to describe behaviour in more objective terms. What does the behaviour look like? What is involved with the behaviour itself?

> "Your voice is raised, and you are pointing your finger in my face. I feel threatened by this kind of behaviour."

A useful exercise to develop clarity about what kinds of behaviour might constitute bullying is to ask people to name specific kinds of behaviour under subjective headings. Normally people describe the following behaviours as forms of bullying.

1. Intimidating behaviour

This involves behaviour that provokes fear. It may be intentional or unintentional. It is normally considered an overt form of bullying. The most common forms of intimidating behaviour are:

- yelling or shouting

- hostile displays of aggression, including throwing things, slamming doors, etc
- verbal or physical threats
- false or exaggerated accusations
- invasion of personal space.

2. Demeaning behaviour

Demeaning behaviour is focused on causing humiliation and embarrassment. It is an attack on a person's self-esteem and is described in domestic violence research as emotional abuse. This can involve:

- belittling comments or gestures
- insults and put-downs
- derogatory name-calling
- condescending behaviour – being patronised or talked down to
- teasing, taunting, and unwanted practical jokes
- being criticised in front of others when it's unnecessary.

3. Undermining behaviour

Behaviour that undermines people is often referred to as a form of covert bullying. It can sometimes occur without the target knowing. It can be very subtle and involve the undermining of a person's standing in an organisation. It may involve:

- unnecessary micro-managing
- gossip, bad-mouthing, spreading damaging rumours
- being questioned unnecessarily
- constant unnecessary criticism
- sabotage or unnecessary disruption of work projects
- setting unreasonable tasks or deadlines
- unwarranted blaming or negative characterising
- taking credit for someone else's work or not giving credit when it is due.

4. Isolating behaviour

Isolating and excluding are very common covert forms of bullying. They either shut a person in and confine them unnecessarily, or they shut a person out and prevent them from access to people, information and resources. The most common forms of this are:

- being ignored and frozen out
- exclusion from meetings, information, resources or support
- being singled out unfairly

- being blamed unfairly or made accountable for the actions of others
- not being given feedback or given credit for good work
- not being given a chance to respond to accusations
- being talked over and shut down unfairly.

5. Victimising behaviour

Behaviour in this realm includes:

- unfair performance appraisals
- being denied procedural fairness
- unfair investigative findings
- unfair disciplinary actions
- unfair sanctioning or requirements
- unfair removal of responsibility.

In summary, these 5 categories assist people to identify the specific types of unreasonable behaviour "within the range" of bullying. If there is repetition within the range of these types of behaviour, then we might say that a person has been bullied. A single incident of any of these behaviours may not amount to bullying.

¶4-040 Behavioural continuum

Behaviour in the workplace can be considered on a continuum. At one end of the continuum is behaviour we want to encourage (positively regarded), and at the other end is behaviour we want to discourage (negatively regarded). On the positive end are behaviours that align with or uphold an organisation's values. On the negative end are behaviours that undermine those values.

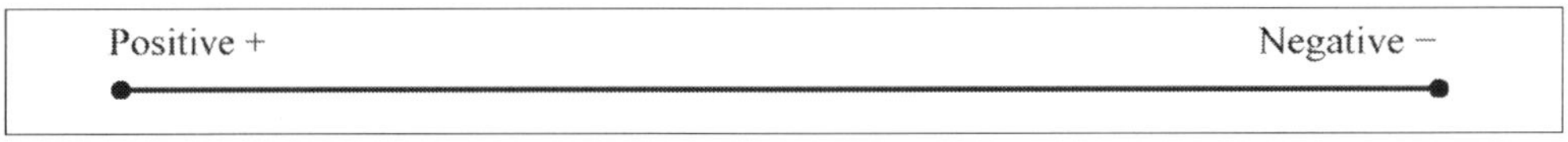

If you ask a group of people to describe 5 types of behaviour they like and appreciate from others, and 5 types of behaviour that they do not like or appreciate, you will find people identify a wide range of behaviours. However, we all share similar views when it comes to behaviour we like and do not like. For example, most people like to be valued and appreciated for what they do, and most people dislike being threatened or humiliated.

Let us take this another step. Suppose you ask people to identify types of behaviour they most like and place them on the continuum toward the positive end. Then ask them to identify behaviour they dislike and place them toward the negative end. Although there is some commonality about the extreme ends of the continuum, when it come to the middle area there is usually a significant amount of variation of opinion.

One thing that comes from this exercise is that people usually put behaviour associated with bullying and harassment at the negative end of the continuum. Most people do not like to be bullied or harassed and consider it destructive behaviour, along with other things such as dishonesty, sabotage and theft.

However, in the centre area types of behaviour will be found that people are indifferent to or that they find annoying or difficult but not necessarily examples of bullying or harassment.

Here is an example of a group's completed behavioural exercise.

Positive + ———————————————— Negative –

Valued behaviour	Difficult behaviour	Destructive behaviour
Constructive feedback Saying thanks Open, honest, frank Listened to Friendliness Sense of humour Supportiveness	Abruptness Grumpiness Quietness Not pulling your weight Unclear requests Argumentative Not taking responsibility	Intimidation Bad mouthing, gossip Unfair exclusion Cruel words Unrealistic demands Set up to fail Public humiliation

By creating a distinction between the "difficult behaviour" list and the "destructive behaviour" list, we might then ask, "Where is the distinguishing line between these two categories of behaviour?"

It may be difficult to decide where that line should be. One way of thinking about this is to consider what sort of behaviour a person should not have to accept or tolerate and what behaviour people should have some tolerance for.

Destructive behaviour is unnecessary and unreasonable. People should not accept or tolerate this behaviour, because it can be harmful.

Difficult behaviour may irritate, annoy or frustrate people but is not significantly destructive. We need to show some tolerance, because we are all human and sometimes we don't behave at our best.

In some work groups this exercise creates a clear list of "above the line" behaviour and "below the line" behaviour. Some groups have even put a visual display on the wall to remind everyone of what behaviour is above or below the line of acceptability.

This allows people to call out behaviour and say, "That's below the line behaviour" or thank people for displaying "above the line behaviour".

This kind of exercise assists people to become aware of how behaviour affects others. It also allows people to consider their own behaviour and how others may be affected by it. In a workplace, having some clarity about the differences between difficult and destructive behaviour creates greater awareness.

A manager briefed his team after training on bullying and harassment:

> "It is important to realise that we are all different and sometimes we may not always appreciate the way people behave toward us in this workplace. You may find at times people criticise what you do and find fault. That is because improvement and learning are what makes us good at what we do. You will not always get what you want here. Your fantastic ideas may not be accepted at first. You need to realise that people have good days and bad days, just like you. They won't always appreciate your wonderful personality and they won't necessarily want to be your friend. Neither do they have to. This is a workplace not a friendship club, and we are here to achieve things, and that means working together and making things work for the overall benefit of the organisation. Things will go wrong, and people will sometimes be upset and frustrated. Hopefully that will be rare, but none of us are perfect. You will need to tolerate and accept some forms of behaviour you find difficult. However, you should never tolerate bullying or harassment. We do not accept acts of intimidation, humiliation, or victimisation as ways of interacting. Undermining people, setting them up to fail, and unfair isolation and exclusion are never acceptable. If that sort of behaviour happens, then you need to speak up and we need to stop it happening again. We are all in this together and we all need to take care of how we affect each other. No one has the right to bully or harass anyone else."

¶4-050 Up, down and sideways

Bullying can happen in all directions. The most common form of bullying, according to the 0800 ZEROBULLY helpline, is downward from a position of authority (67%). It is common for people with positional authority to feel entitled to bully as a means of control. It is not uncommon to hear of someone who has started bullying people after being promoted to a supervisory level. This may be because the new manager or team leader is unfamiliar with holding positional authority. They may have insufficient tools to manage people or no longer empathise with those below them. This is a common phenomenon.

Bullying downwards is sometimes seen as a privilege associated with positional power:

> "I am the boss. I will do as I like."

However, positional power does not confer the right to bully. When people begin to see positional authority as a responsibility, rather than a privilege, this notion that bullying is a right of the mighty diminishes.

The next most common form of bullying is peer or horizontal bullying. In the nursing profession, the term, "horizontal violence" describes a very common type of peer bullying. Nurses have commonly talked about their profession in a dramatic way:

> "We are the only profession that eat our young."

This describes a dynamic that involves the senior nurse bullying the junior nurse, who then, after surviving the torment, inflicts the same treatment on the next intake. Like domestic violence, there is a generational effect that keeps this dynamic occurring. Like a rite of passage, the people who do this keep it happening. This doesn't just happen in nursing but in many professions, such as police, fire and ambulance workers, trades, hospitality and service industries. The bullied become the next generation of bullies:

> "It happened to me and that's why it's happening to you."
>
> "You're not a real nurse until you have had to experience this."

The least common form of bullying is upwards bullying. It is also the least recognised. This is when people bully their supervisors, and it often involves group tactics or mobbing. Typical forms of upwards bullying involve:

- refusals to communicate or cooperate
- withholding information
- creating unnecessary disruption
- aggressive communication
- false accusations of bullying or other inappropriate behaviour
- sabotage of work or equipment
- undermining by spreading false rumours.

Often this happens to the new manager who has recently taken over from a manager who bullied or allowed bullying to occur. The team has become hardened and protective. They now turn on the new manager and bully upwards.

Managers who face this kind of behaviour need to recognise it as a form of bullying. They may require support to protect themselves and address the behavioural dynamics that are occurring. Managers who face upward bullying need to try and form relationships with individuals in the mob to change this dynamic. Once relationships have developed, the manager can then begin to challenge the bullying. It is useful to start conversations about past behaviour and how the team developed their ways of behaving. It is also important to name the types of behaviour involved and create new agreements for behaviour and interaction. It may be a difficult test for a new manager to address this kind of dynamic. If the manager reacts and uses defensive and demanding behaviour, this will reinforce the dynamics and make things even more difficult. Upward bullying can be very difficult to prove by investigation, because the mob will generally not speak up against each other. Therefore, taking matters through a complaints process may be unproductive.

Chapter 5

How People and Organisations Are Affected by Bullying and Harassment

¶5-010 The impact of bullying and harassment

The impact of bullying and harassment on people can vary significantly. Some people show a remarkable ability to endure prolonged destructive behaviour. Others can be traumatised and suffer physical and psychological injury after only a relatively short time of exposure.

In the initial stages, targets often experience shock and bewilderment. They might be alarmed by the behaviour, but they usually focus on trying to restore normality. This period is the best time for restorative interventions to be made.

However, as time goes on, if the adverse situations continue, targets may go through a deteriorating spiral. This starts with increased levels of anxiety and hypervigilance and may develop into despair and depression. The cumulative impact of repeated exposure to this behaviour can be highly destructive on individuals and may even lead to post traumatic stress disorder (PTSD), suicide and even homicide. The term "going postal" describes a phenomenon where targets of bullying have resorted to murdering the people who have bullied them.

Targets can also experience a shift in their mindsets. Initially they might be interested in resolving matters and getting the bullying to stop, but then they move to either wanting to flee the workplace or fighting back and getting justice by some means. Sometimes they seek to achieve that justice by going to media with accusations of being bullied, posting online accusations, and slandering their alleged bullies. Revenge in the public arena can be sweet for some people who have not received justice from their employer. Bullying and harassment are volatile issues, and unless employers treat them seriously the damage caused by unresolved grievances can be substantial.

¶5-020 Eroding self-confidence

One of the most common effects of bullying is damage to self-esteem and confidence. Targets may interpret what is happening to them as if they have somehow contributed to it, caused it, or deserve it in some way. This self-doubt can be pervasive and may lead to a deterioration of their psychological state, rendering them less able to stand up to further exposure.

With bullying and harassment, the first impact may be physical and emotional, and the second impact may have deeper psychological effects, which is where the danger really lies. It is in the interpretation of events that beliefs are formed about oneself:

> "It's not what happens to you that affects you as much as the meaning you attach to what has happened to you."

Once a target has begun to doubt themselves or take responsibility in some way for the behaviour of another person, this can become like a worm in their psyche. That self-doubt can take a person down a perilous route that destroys their self-confidence and even their life force:

> "What's wrong with me that I have been bullied, and what's wrong with me that I have not been able to stop it."

Perpetrators will often avoid responsibility and accountability. Their pattern of behaviour has developed over time and becomes ingrained. They will employ certain tactics to avoid responsibility. Tactics such as minimisation, denial and blame serve perpetrators well and they can also develop powerful gaslighting skills and aggressive "doubling down" to protect themselves from scrutiny and the need to change.

¶5-030 Gaslighting

The term "gaslighting" has become far more familiar in recent times. The term comes from a 1944 movie called "Gaslight" in which a husband uses trickery to convince his wife that she is mentally unwell so he can steal from her. [1] In the movie, the husband adjusts the light from the gas lighting system, and when his wife mentions that the lighting has changed, he denies it and questions her ability to accurately assess the situation.

Gaslighting describes the way in which the perpetrator attempts to manipulate the target, causing them to doubt the validity of their own personal experience. Instead, they are manipulated to agree with the perpetrator's narrative that insists they are wrong and that their emotional reaction is irrational or dysfunctional. It is more than simply disagreeing about something. The impact of gaslighting is that the target begins to consistently doubt themselves and becomes more attached to the perpetrator's view and beliefs.

¶5-040 Fight or flight

The "fight or flight" response is an automatic physiological response to threats. The perception of threat activates the sympathetic nervous system, and this triggers a stress response in the body. Typically, this involves:

1 Thomas, Laura (2018), "*Gaslight* and gaslighting", *The Lancet Psychiatry* **5** (2): 117–118 (February 2018).

- increased heart rate and blood pressure
- adrenalin and cortisol activation in the bloodstream
- dilation of pupils
- skin flushes
- increased energy and breathing
- trembling.

These physical reactions prepare the body to fight back or to flee from what is perceived as threatening. It can also involve "freezing", where the person cannot move and will even stop breathing momentarily in response to the perceived threat, like a rabbit in the headlights.

These responses are powerful, and when a person is regularly experiencing them, it can take a considerable toll on their psychological and physical health. It is important to note that these responses are triggered by the perception of a threat. This explains why reactions differ when different people encounter the same situations. People do not perceive the same threat in the same way.

¶5-050 Long-term signs

The impact of continued exposure to bullying and harassment can be severe. When a person repeatedly experiences the "fight or flight" reaction in their bodies, it can lead to serious physical, psychological and behavioural symptoms.

Physical body signs can include:

- high blood pressure
- cardiovascular conditions
- headaches
- muscular pain
- skin rashes
- digestive problems
- hair loss

Psychological and emotional signs can include:

- exhaustion/burnout
- anxiety/panic attacks
- obsessive thinking
- hypervigilance
- anger and vengeful thoughts
- irrationality
- memory loss.

Behavioural symptoms can include:

- withdrawal
- sleeplessness
- bouts of anger that can be expressed toward family and friends
- overuse of alcohol or drugs
- self-harming.

These symptoms may develop gradually and increase in potency and become debilitating over time.

¶5-060 Organisational impact

When bullying or harassment happen in a work team, the culture begins to change in a characteristic and predictable way. If it is not addressed early, there will be a slide into a set of dynamics that will embed the destructive behaviours. This will make addressing them far more difficult in the future. It can be like a shadow that descends over a work group.

In a healthy work team, when someone bullies or harasses, people speak up and address it quickly. The most common process is informal, and the matter is often resolved without much disturbance. Perpetrators take responsibility and make amends because they are faced with the results of their behaviour. If not, they leave, because the workplace will not allow unresolved issues to fester. When they bully, the spotlight falls on them rather than their targets. They are called to account, and a shadow does not develop.

However, when early intervention does not happen, specific changes can occur.

Firstly, people begin to polarise into groups. Some will support the perpetrators and their behaviour, and will act to protect them from accountability. Some will copy their behaviour and may become sycophantic in their allegiance. This forms a bullying mob. Other people will polarise toward the targets of the bullying and harassment. They support the targets and may also protect the targets from further abuse. This is the protector mob.

Some people will be caught in the middle. They see what's happening, but they want to keep themselves safe. They become inactive participants who try not to get involved, but in their neutrality they "turn a blind eye" and passively collude with what is happening.

As time goes on, this polarisation can increase, and at its worst people are forced to take sides. They will either join the mob that supports the bullying and harassment or join the mob that supports the targets. Eventually the oppressed (targets) may even become oppressors as they fight back and turn the tables through sabotage and disruption. In the end, it may not be clear who is the bully or who is the target, as everyone becomes complicit and caught up in the dynamics.

This polarising effect is called the "Us and Them" dynamic. Bullying creates polarisation and fragmentation in groups.

Another thing that occurs is the "climate of fear" dynamic. People become less trusting and more insecure. Things become more unpredictable and chaotic. People shift from being generative and creative to focusing on how to cope and survive. In the shadow, life is arduous and difficult. The climate of fear ensures that people toe the line.

This dynamic is exacerbated when those in authority act without responsibility and accountability. Some perpetrators will create this dynamic in a calculating and systematic way because this environment allows them to avoid accountability for their destructive behaviour. They seek power and control by provoking fear and insecurity.

In a workplace where there is a climate of fear, people do not complain about bullying and harassment. It is unsafe to do so. Instead, they become hardened, or they leave.

Another dynamic that develops in workgroups afflicted with bullying and harassment is the dynamic of acceptance. Bullying behaviour becomes accepted as normal. People do not call bullying or harassing behaviours by their names. They are renamed into more palatable terms. Abusive displays of anger become expressions of passion and strength. Harassment is seen as fun and banter. Undermining is being politically savvy. Lies and disinformation become the new truths. Anyone who speaks out is considered a traitor to the leaders, a troublemaker, or disturber of the status quo. A code of silence protects those who bully by demonising the truth-tellers.

Like a toxic shadow, these dynamics begin to develop, slowly at first and then more rapidly. Things become more and more obscure, unreliable, unclear, and confusing, the denser the dynamic of the shadow becomes. People must adapt to survive, but in adapting they usually give up aspects of their own clarity and even sanity.

Organisations that have significant shadows will find it extremely difficult to effect change in the system. Unless the change comes from senior management levels, it is unlikely to happen at all. The problem is that at higher levels the shadow may not be as apparent as at lower levels. Senior management may not understand what is happening further down through the organisation because they do not get accurate information about what is occurring. Alternatively, if the shadow is being generated at senior levels in an organisation its effect will flow down throughout all the other levels.

¶5-070 Removing the shadow

In order to change the dynamics that bullying and harassment create, people need to begin to talk about them. Liberation begins with dialogue. Listening to people and creating a safe forum to talk about what is happening is crucial if there is to be any shift in the dynamics.

This is only the start. There is no single thing that changes a toxic system, as it tends to be multi-layered and complex. It usually requires new people at the most senior levels, because those in the system have probably adapted to it. They will be unlikely to be able to change it. Instead, they tend to recreate the same toxic system. Toxic systems are closed and stagnant because they are focused on protecting the status quo and maintaining power and control.

Trust is a key element that disappears with the shadow. It is replaced by distrust – distrust of management, individuals, information and of investigation and disciplinary processes. The more people distrust, the more they withhold, the more calculating and secretive they become. Therefore, any strategy to bring about change in the system requires trust to be re-established.

To dispel the shadow, people need to create a shift in the dynamics. Instead of "us and them", they need to generate a genuine dynamic of "we". Instead of a climate of fear, there needs to be a climate of safety and trust. Instead of acceptance of bullying and harassing behaviours, there needs to be a genuine rejection of these behaviours.

Whatever an organisation does to shift these dynamics will be beneficial. However, simply trying to change one aspect of the dynamics will usually not succeed in shifting things significantly. The dynamics of the shadow create a system of attitudes and defensive strategies. The solution lies in a multi-pronged strategy of organisational change. It often takes sustained effort to change a system.

Many large organisations start with facilitated educational programmes that allow people to talk about bullying and harassment. This might be followed by a staff survey or focus groups that bring to light what people experience and think about the issue. This may give valuable information about people's confidence in management to deal with concerns or complaints that might be raised. When issues are raised, it is vitally important that managers know how to respond effectively. This requires courage from the top and it may require someone being dismissed before employees begin to believe their senior managers are genuinely committed.

If managers respond defensively, it is likely that people will lose confidence and retreat to the shadow. It is therefore important that managers at all levels have some guidance and education prior to the commencement of staff training. They need to be ready for people to come forward and need to know how to respond effectively.

In addition to managers being trained, an organisation may train specific people who can act as contact persons. These people provide a confidential service, listening to concerns, providing information about options, and assisting enquirers to make decisions about what to do about their concerns. Contact persons need to be equipped to provide a support role to other staff. They can do a lot to help resolve issues without exacerbating situations.

The shadow is a useful metaphor to describe the set of dynamics that bullying and harassment create. When the shadow is weak, there is more possibility of effecting change without disruption. When the shadow is strong, it will require significant efforts and ongoing interventions to create change.

Chapter 6

Why People Bully and Harass and Why They Stop

¶6-010 The bullying and harassment continuum

Anyone can bully or harass. Some do it more than others and some do it more severely than others. Those who bully and harass fit somewhere on a continuum. At one end of the continuum are those occasional or situational bullies or harassers, and at the other end are the chronic bullies and harassers.

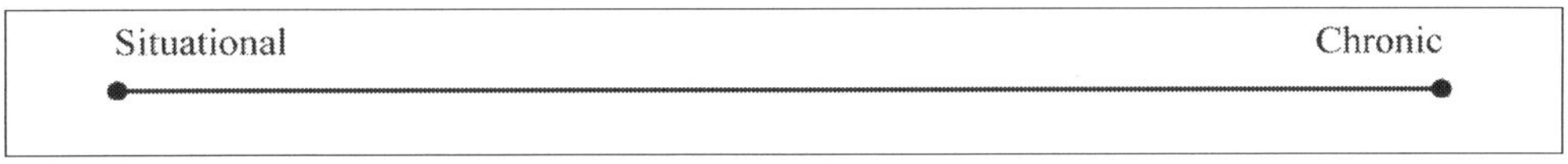

¶6-020 Situational bullies and harassers

Situational bullies and harassers are people who occasionally use bullying or harassing behaviours. In times of high stress or when they are under pressure, they might begin to use bullying tactics. In the case of sexual harassment, they might be guilty of making sexual comments in certain social settings such as the end of year work Christmas party. Situational bullies and harassers are far more common than chronic bullies and harassers. They generate a significant number of complaints in workplaces.

Situational bullies and harassers are more amenable to change when they are at the less severe end of the continuum and have more capacity for empathy and self-awareness. They can self-reflect and change their behaviour if they are committed to doing so and are in a social system that requires accountability.

¶6-030 Chronic bullies and harassers

Chronic or serial bullies and harassers are often recognised by their lack of empathy and self-awareness. At the worst end of the continuum, they are described as having a disordered personality such as psychopathy or sociopathy. They use bullying tactics regularly and have no awareness or do not care if they hurt or damage people. While they may be only 1% of a population, their impact on people and on organisations can be catastrophic.

Dr Robert D Hare, a world recognised expert on psychopathy and the developer of what is known as the Psychopathy Checklist, lists the main symptoms of this personality disorder:[1]

Emotional/Interpersonal	Social Deviance
• Glib and superficial	• Impulsive
• Egocentric and grandiose	• Poor behaviour controls
• Lack of remorse or guilt	• Need for excitement
• Lack of empathy	• Lack of responsibility
• Deceitful and manipulative	• Early behaviour problems
• Shallow emotions	• Adult antisocial behaviour

Dr Hare warns against using the tool without proper training and explains that many people have some of the traits of psychopathy but are not psychopathic. However, he also explains that not all psychopaths are criminals and that they are found in organisations and communities. They are among us whether we like it or not.

One of the characteristics of chronic bullies and harassers (some of whom may be psychopathic) is their resistance to change. While situational bullies can change, chronic bullies do not seem to be able to do so as quickly, if at all. Some people have argued that chronic bullies don't change because they genuinely don't believe they need to change. However, it is more likely that they don't change because people usually avoid calling them out and requiring them to change.

¶6-040 The stool model

The stool model explains what it takes for someone to establish a pattern of bullying or harassing in a social group. A stool with three legs is a strong platform to stand on, but each leg on its own is relatively weak. In this model each leg is an aspect that supports the continuance of bullying and harassment.

The first leg is described as a "sense of entitlement". People bully on the basis that they are entitled to do so. They find a reason externally or internally that provides a justification for their bullying behaviour. Some common entitlement positions are:

- I have authority over you.
- You deserve it.
- You irritate me.
- You are not performing the way I want.

1 Hare, Robert D, *Without Conscience: The Disturbing World of Psychopaths Among Us*, Guilford Press (1993). p 34.

- I am in a bad mood and can take it out on you.
- I bully because I can get away with it.

The second leg of the stool model is a "lack of empathy". When people bully, they lack empathy. They view the target as an object and dehumanise them.

Empathy prevents people from bullying and using any form of violence. It is very difficult to hurt someone if you are identifying with the pain or fear of the person you are hurting. Empathy gets in the way of violence because it connects us to another person and their experience.

This is why, in war, the enemy is often portrayed as "dirty rats" or some other object of disgust. It is easier for soldiers to kill rats than human beings.

The third leg of the stool model is "untouchableness". For a person to continue to bully or harass, they must find a way to stop other people in the social system from challenging their behaviour. They must become untouchable. How do they do this? They create a shadow around themselves – a climate of fear, of acceptance, a code of silence and an "Us and Them" dynamic. Initially the bullying may occur where there are no witnesses, but as time goes on, the bullying will usually become more public and more obvious. Perpetrators will employ tactics of blame, denial, minimisation. If that doesn't work, then threats and coercion will be added. They will groom others to turn a blind eye and recruit others to support their behaviour, endorse their bullying, and even bully on their behalf. Chronic bullies and harassers are usually skilled in the art of manipulating others. They bully because people stop holding them to account.

¶6-050 How do bullies change?

The stool model offers insight into what it takes to stop bullying. The 3-legged stool is a strong platform, but if the legs are reduced then it becomes less stable. A 2-legged stool is very unstable and a one-legged stool even more so.

When the leg of untouchableness is removed, people will be challenged when they bully. They will be called to account for their behaviour and face consequences as a result.

> In one small business, the owner/operator regularly bullied his staff. He was known for his impatience and his verbal abuse. He sometimes threw tools in the workshop and often yelled and swore at people when he was upset. The staff met together and discussed what to do about it. They told the owner that they would no longer accept his abusive behaviour. They warned him that when it occurred they would stop work and meet in the staff room. They would not return to work until he had acknowledged his behaviour was unacceptable and made amends. The team used this intervention, and this was enough for the owner to change his behaviour.

Removing the legs of entitlement and lack of empathy often requires some specific interventions. When a perpetrator must face the person they have injured and understand the effect of their behaviour, this can be a powerful intervention that creates empathy. In restorative practices, the perpetrator must listen to the person they have hurt. They become involved and accountable.

> At a work social event a manager became intoxicated and sexually assaulted a co-worker. The incident was witnessed and reported, and the manager was reprimanded and given a written warning. The manager was told that her behaviour had impacted the management team. They had lost confidence in her and had considered dismissing her. In a courageous move she asked to meet with the management team. An external facilitator was employed to conduct a restorative session. In the session the manager expressed her remorse and asked the group of managers to express themselves honestly about her transgression. Each manager expressed their anger and disappointment. They also expressed their fears and concerns about the use of alcohol at events. The manager received each person's comments without attempting to excuse her behaviour. The process achieved three outcomes. The accused manager took responsibility for her behaviour and entered a rehabilitation programme. The management group moved from anger and outrage to a more empathetic and supportive position. The management team also created a responsible alcohol policy for future events.

The key catalyst for change is empathy. Perpetrators will often begin to change when they are brought face to face with the person they have hurt. They begin to identify with the experience of the target, and they understand the effect of their behaviour. If this intervention doesn't work, the perpetrator may require significant therapy to develop empathy.

Dr Laura Crawshaw (aka The Boss Whisperer) describes in her book *Taming the Abrasive Manager*, that empathy can be learned, even in later life. She explains that abrasive managers do what they do because they do not understand or read emotions:

> "If these emotionally blind bosses can be made to see what they do, there's a very good chance that they will begin to care enough to stop doing it."[2]

If an organisation aims to prevent bullying and harassment, it needs a strategy that focuses on reducing the strength of all 3 legs of the stool model. An organisation can take steps to remove the sense of entitlement by using various educational processes. It can create work programmes that emphasise that no one is entitled to bully or harass and that these behaviours are never

2 Crawshaw, Laura, *Taming the Abrasive Manager. How to End Unnecessary Roughness in the Workplace*, Jossey-Bass (2007), p 94.

acceptable. This is more than a zero-tolerance policy, it is a prevention policy. These messages need to become part of organisational values and the organisation's ongoing goals for future social and cultural development.

Organisations can develop processes to address bullying and harassment that emphasise the development of empathy. They can also discourage untouchableness by emphasising that everyone is accountable for their behaviour.

Unfortunately, the dominant paradigm in many organisations is to create a zero-tolerance policy and expect people to report bullying and harassment. This is followed by investigation and disciplinary processes that separate perpetrators from their targets. It involves written submissions, establishing evidence to prove guilt, and arguing over whether allegations have sufficient substance. The organisation's risk can become the central focus, and little is done to create empathy and restore relationships.

Chapter 7

Options to Resolve Bullying and Harassment

¶7-010 The 3 main options

People who get bullied and harassed in organisations usually have 3 main options to address matters. These are:

- self-help
- informal intervention
- formal complaint.

Each option has a different process and involves different people. Each option has its own advantages and disadvantages. There is no "right" way. Any option can be appropriate.

Self-help	The target seeks to stop the bullying and harassment by direct communication with the perpetrator. Action is also taken by the target to protect themselves from further harm.
Informal intervention	The target engages with a third party who intervenes to stop the bullying or harassment. The third-party is usually a manager above the perpetrator. Third parties may also include mediators or facilitators; however, it is the manager's role to ensure the bullying or harassment stops.
Formal complaint	The target makes a complaint. Complaints are investigated by senior management or external investigators. If sufficient evidence is found, the matter proceeds to a disciplinary process.

These are "in-house" options. Other, external options are also possible, such as raising the matter with WorkSafe or the Human Rights Commission (New Zealand), the Fair Work Commission (Australia), or the police in some cases.

¶7-020 Self-help option

People who are bullied or harassed usually try to resolve matters on their own during the initial stages. They will seek to protect themselves by avoiding contact with the perpetrator or by defending and protecting themselves in some way from further suffering. They might confront or challenge the perpetrator, but their capacity to do so depends on their own inner resources, confidence and skills. It also depends upon external factors such as the social system, the social standing of the perpetrator, including their position and authority, and the commitment of management to address bullying and harassment.

Sometimes the target may resort to aggression or reciprocal bullying to stop the bullying or harassment. This is not uncommon in New Zealand and Australian workplaces. When asking participants in a training session about what they might do if they were bullied, there is usually someone who says something like:

> "A punch on the nose usually works well."

Maybe there is something in our pioneering culture that sees this kind of response as appropriate. It is common for people to think that violence or reciprocal bullying is an option. However, this usually creates more problems than it solves.

In one workplace dining room, a sign hung on the wall that read:

> "In a good workplace, the rule is do unto others as you would have them do unto you, but in this workplace the rule is DO OTHERS BEFORE THEY DO YOU."

This kind of combative stance indicates a toxic workplace culture and will only serve to encourage bullying as a means of survival. Once this type of culture is accepted as normal, bullying and harassment become the norm.

Sometimes when a target stands strong and presents themselves with confidence, a perpetrator may back down. They realise the target will not be easily bullied. Power doesn't need to be expressed in the form of violence.

The most common response to bullying is to avoid encounters with the perpetrator. This can be disruptive to work and can empower the perpetrator. It may or may not reduce the likelihood of further bullying.

Other common protective tactics include:

- avoiding contact with the perpetrator
- demanding a witness to any closed-door meetings with the perpetrator
- withdrawing and disengaging when the perpetrator is present
- refusing to engage or share information or resources with the perpetrator.

These tactics are disruptive to the functioning of a group. They put a strain on relationships and create roadblocks to communication. Some people maintain that a target has the right to act in the interests of their own health and safety by using these tactics. However, they do not resolve issues between people and tend to create more problems in the longer term.

Targets can document incidents and use email to create records of interactions. They sometimes resort to recording incidents using a voice recorder or video app on their cell phones. This form of evidence collection might later be used to support a formal complaint.

A more direct form of self-help is to speak up and initiate a "courageous conversation" with the perpetrator.

¶7-030 Courageous conversations

Typically, the courageous conversation lets the recipient know that their behaviour is unwanted and unreasonable and that it needs to stop. People may find it useful to describe the behaviour so that the perpetrator understands specifically what they have done to cause offence. It can be useful to describe the effect of that behaviour as well. When these 2 aspects are presented, a powerful outcome can be created for the target. This approach can also create a favourable outcome for the perpetrator, who may not have understood how their behaviour has been experienced. One team leader said:

> "I didn't realise that one of my staff felt bullied by me. He let me know in private after an incident. I was taken aback but I also respected the person's guts to challenge me. We get on a lot better now and I have changed because of that."

A courageous conversation can have three aspects:

1. describe the behaviour in an observable way
2. describe the effect of that behaviour
3. state a preferred way of behaving that is more reasonable.

What does it mean to describe behaviour in an observable way? It means to name it as it appears to someone observing it, rather than adding meaning or judgment to it.

"I don't appreciate being yelled at" is observational.

"I don't appreciate being bullied" is not observational and doesn't let the person know the specific kind of behaviour involved.

When describing an effect, a person can describe an emotion or feeling, but they could also describe other effects.

"When you yell at me, I feel intimidated" describes an emotional effect.

"When you yell at me, I stop listening to you" describes a behavioural effect.

"When you yell at me, I lose respect for you" describes a psychological effect.

This allows the other person to develop empathy, which can be quite useful:

> "I didn't realise you felt that way. I'm sorry for causing that."

When describing the preferred or more reasonable behaviour, a person can also say what they want rather than what they don't want. This gives the other person valuable information about the behaviour that is preferred.

> "Can you please keep your voice down; I don't appreciate being yelled at."

This is clear and useful communication, and the courageous conversation may even start with a request for preferred behaviour. The goal is to convey an accurate and clear message.

It is also important to think about the way the message is conveyed: the sound of it, the tone of it. It needs to ring true and be consistent to be powerful, without being aggressive.

> "I realise that you have a lot going on and your job is stressful. However, I find that when your voice gets raised I tend to back off and feel quite resentful... (pause and give time for person to respond)... I would appreciate it if you would speak in a calm way without yelling at me. That would help me understand what you want, and we will get on a lot better."

There is no guarantee that a courageous conversation will produce a desirable outcome. However, it provides a constructive platform.

Self-help options work best when there is an environment or culture that has the following features:

- strong, cohesive relationships between people
- high levels of trust and support
- beneficial working relationships and constructive feedback
- ongoing education and training on communication and bullying/harassment prevention
- emotional intelligence competencies
- personal accountability.

When there is a lack of other options to resolve issues, the self-help option may be the only possibility for a target. If management are not interested in assisting people or lack the resources to respond effectively, targets will resort to self-help options. Unfortunately, the most common "self-help" action people take is to leave the workplace. The more toxic a workplace culture, the more people will leave.

Managers need to foster a culture where direct communication is the norm. They need to value feedback and both give and receive it. In this way issues can be raised early and resolved before they develop into complaints and formal processes.

¶7-040 Informal intervention option

Informal interventions are sometimes described as a "no-blame" approach to resolving bullying or harassment. They involve a third-party who helps resolve matters without the need for formal investigations or disciplinary approaches.

Informal interventions are normally conducted by managers or supervisors, and sometimes they involve the assistance of a mediator or facilitator. This is a growing area of speciality within workplaces, and there are different ways that informal interventions can be conducted.

In short, informal interventions involve 5 phases:

Phase 1:	The "concerned person" informs a manager of their concerns about bullying or harassment.
Phase 2:	The manager conducts an exploratory conversation (see EXPLORE model) with the concerned person and an intervention plan is devised.
Phase 3:	The manager informs the other person (the "person concerned") that concerns have been raised and a discussion ensues to resolve matters.
Phase 4:	A resolution process is conducted, and agreements are made between parties.
Phase 5:	Agreements are monitored and managed into the future. Support is provided to ensure the prevention of bullying and harassment, as well as improvement of the relationship.

Informal interventions differ from formal complaint processes. As a "no-blame" approach, they do not result in written allegations being kept on record that could disadvantage someone. The process is not disadvantageous to any party involved. Steps are taken to ensure that no one is blamed or treated as a perpetrator or a victim.

Traditional mediation where 2 people sit around a table with a mediator is one form of informal intervention but is not the only form. Sometimes traditional mediation is inappropriate and can result in further trauma for the target.

Types of informal interventions:

- manager-directed resolutions
- facilitated discussions
- direct or face-to-face mediation
- round-table facilitation.

In addition to this, there may be interventions such as:

- training, coaching, mentoring
- team reviews.

¶7-050 Importance of language

Informal interventions should involve different languages than formal processes, so as not to confuse people. This is important to ensure the informal process is not contaminated with a formal process. When contamination occurs between these 2 processes, it can result in people becoming confused, losing trust, and resorting to adversarial tactics.

For example, there is no such thing as an informal complaint. Complaints are always formal. This kind of language is confusing. If a person perceives they are facing formal disciplinary proceedings or that records will be held that indicate a complaint has been made, they will usually want everything in writing and may ensure they have their own legal counsel. The chance of being able to have open communication and resolution quickly disappears.

Therefore, the person who initially raises concerns with a manager is called the "concerned person", not the victim, target or complainant. The person they are concerned about is called the "person concerned", not the bully, harasser, respondent or perpetrator.

Instead of talking about "complaints", we talk about "concerns" that have been raised. There is no investigation, but there is an "exploration" of the matter. There are no findings, but there are "conclusions and agreements." There are no records of allegations, but there may be a record of agreements.

If we want people to "buy in" to informal interventions, the process needs to be fair and safe. It should not disadvantage anyone. It is an alternative to formal complaints, investigations, and the threat of disciplinary action. This should be advantageous to everyone concerned.

Those who bully or harass can learn something from this process. They can develop more understanding and empathy and choose more constructive behaviour. They can also avoid the pain of going through a lengthy formal investigation process that might lead to potential disciplinary outcomes. Those who have been bullied or harassed can be heard and understood and can achieve the changes they want. They can also feel satisfied because they have acted to resolve matters, not to elevate them to a more adversarial level.

When targets raise concerns and are asked about what they would like to see happen, they commonly just want the inappropriate behaviour to stop. However, once a formal process has begun, or concerns are put into writing, the dynamics usually take on a more threatening tone. People become more defensive and adversarial.

¶7-060 What happens if informal interventions fail?

Informal interventions may not be successful in stopping bullying or harassment. Sometimes people may change inappropriate behaviour for a few weeks and then resort to their old patterns. For this reason, it is important to monitor the situation and assist both parties in terms of coaching, training or behavioural modification.

If either party does not honour the agreement made in an informal process, the other party may choose to make a formal complaint. If a complaint is initiated after a failed informal intervention, the investigator will need to be someone independent, that is, someone who has not heard any privileged information raised during the informal intervention.

¶7-070 Shouldn't concerns always be reported in writing?

The problem with recording every concern that is raised is that once it has been put in writing the concern will usually be perceived as a complaint. People respond differently to the word "complaint" than they do to the word "concern". They respond differently to things put to them in writing rather than put to them verbally.

> "I want to raise something with you. I want you to know that some concerns have been raised with me that concern you. They have been raised with the hope of resolving matters amicably. They have not been put in writing. This is not a formal complaint, but it could go that way if this is not resolved in an informal way. Can I discuss these concerns with you?"

There is another problem with putting concerns in writing: the focus shifts from sorting things out to proving that the concerns are real. It becomes a matter of proving allegations. This can only be done by undertaking an investigation.

Is it necessary to prove every allegation of bullying and harassment? No. The priority needs to be ensuring people are safe and secure and that bullying and harassment do not continue. Informal processes are focused on resolving concerns. Formal processes are focused on proving allegations.

By reporting every concern in writing, we lessen the likelihood of resolving those concerns. It becomes a distraction and people become adversarial. It is then far more difficult to get people communicating, taking responsibility, and making gestures of reconciliation.

> "You can catch more flies with honey than with vinegar."

Imagine a situation where you are told that another person has raised some concerns about you and wants to resolve the situation in a fair and reasonable way. You are told that this person has chosen not to make a formal complaint but is hoping that there might be a more mutually beneficial way to resolve matters involving a third party.

How would you respond to that? Would it be different than receiving a written allegation of bullying or harassment?

Maybe your initial reaction might be defensive and aggressive, especially if you know it is a difficult relationship. You might initially react with denial and counter-allegation. But when you realise that a complaint hasn't been made and the request is to sort things out, you might consider the beneficial aspect of that. If you realise that the matter may get elevated to a formal complaint if it is not resolved, you may prefer to go through an informal process.

Complaints by their nature are adversarial. When a person makes a complaint against someone it is "against" them. The person who receives the complaint will defend themselves "against" the complaint. Both people are involved in acting "against" something. This is the very definition of "adversarial". People become pitted against each other.

In some organisations people immediately call their lawyers and take actions that are not conducive to resolving matters. Common adversarial responses include:

- refusing to acknowledge responsibility (don't admit liability)
- counter-complaining (attack is the best method of defence)
- delaying (obfuscation)
- ignoring (it's been dealt with)
- diverting attention ("but what about. . .?").

These tactics reduce the chance of resolution. They do not bring people together but force them further apart. Formal processes are necessary but only when it might be necessary to remove someone. It should not be the automatic response whenever someone raises concerns.

At an organisational level, the "putting into writing" of every concern will create a climate of fear, where people will eventually stop raising concerns. It may increase the number of complaints and investigations. Some people will use complaints as an opportunity to disrupt and retaliate against people they dislike. The organisation will shift from a prevention culture to an adversarial culture.

¶7-080 External helplines

Some organisations provide an external helpline for staff to call and anonymously report bullying and harassment. This makes it easy for people to speak up and can be useful in some cases by alerting senior management to problems. However, there are some significant issues with this kind of process.

Anonymous complaints cannot be used to determine whether bullying or harassment is occurring. An employer cannot determine whether the reporting is accurate, even where multiple reports are made from the same area about the same alleged perpetrator.

The principles of natural justice must prevail. An accused person has the right to know who their accuser is. They also have the right to defend themselves against allegations and therefore they need to know the details, including the identity of the person making the allegations.

Allowing an anonymous form of reporting can be abused by those who seek to bully others. False allegations are a form of bullying. Some people will abuse a helpline to defame others. If the organisation allows this or holds anonymous allegations against a person, there may be a risk of this information being "discovered". This can make the organisation vulnerable to claims of unfairness and disadvantage.

The main benefit that helplines provide is to engage with the person reporting and offer some form of advice. This may assist the person to undertake one of the 3 options (self-help, informal, formal) available to resolve matters.

The other benefit that helplines provide is that they alert senior management to potential bullying or harassment hazards. Based on reports, management might focus attention on a work team and explore the dynamics in the team through a team review.

¶7-090 Formal complaint option

When a formal complaint is made, the first responsibility of an employer is to investigate the complaint to ascertain its validity. This can create problems that complainants usually do not anticipate.

Formal complaints are sometimes necessary. They are the only way an organisation can form the evidential basis to take disciplinary action against a perpetrator. This action might result in a written warning when matters are found to reach the level of misconduct. It might result in summary dismissal when matters have reached the level of serious misconduct. Bullying and harassment can constitute either misconduct or serious misconduct, depending on the seriousness of behaviour, the intentions of the perpetrator, and the persistence of the perpetrator's inappropriate behaviour.

An organisation needs to have a clear, established process for managing formal complaints of bullying and harassment. Those who investigate complaints should do so fairly without bias or predetermination. Findings need to be clearly determined on evidence, not on opinions or hearsay. There should be a written final report showing how the investigator reached the findings. Everything must be done transparently and thoroughly, because the process and findings may later be challenged in a court.

A typical process for investigating complaints of bullying or harassment involves specific stages, including:

Stage 1:	A concerned person informs a manager of their concerns about bullying or harassment.
Stage 2:	The manager conducts an exploratory conversation (see EXPLORE model) with the concerned person. A conclusion is reached to proceed with a formal complaint. Allegations are documented.
Stage 3:	An investigator is appointed, and the terms of reference or scope of the investigation are determined.
Stage 4:	The investigator interviews the complainant and produces a written account of the interview, clarifying the specific allegations of bullying or harassment.
Stage 5:	The respondent (person being complained about) is provided with the written allegations, the complainant's interview notes, the terms of reference and other important information about the possible outcomes of the investigation. Safety and support measures need to be discussed with the respondent. The potential for disciplinary action and/or dismissal needs to be explained.
Stage 6:	The investigator interviews the respondent and creates a written account of the interview, including specific responses to the allegations of the complainant.
Stage 7:	If the allegations are accepted by the respondent, the investigator may conclude the investigation. However, if there is a dispute or denial of the allegations, the investigator will need to examine other potential sources of evidence. This might include interviewing witnesses or examining documentation relating to the complaint. When there are counterclaims, the investigator will need to examine them as well.
Stage 8:	Draft report stage. The investigator gathers all the written material relating to the investigation and provides this to the complainant and the respondent. Each party can view what has been alleged and the responses. The complainant and respondent are allowed to provide further comment or evidence to assist the investigator in making a finding.
Stage 9:	Final Report stage. The investigator, after having weighed all the evidence, including the final submissions of the parties involved, determines a finding. Normally findings are: • The allegations have substance, and the complaint is upheld. • The allegations do not have substance because there is insufficient evidence to uphold the complaint. • The allegations are false.

A completed investigation determines whether the allegations have validity. Once this has been determined, the employer has options:

1. Proceed with disciplinary action against the offending party. This could result in dismissal if the evidence is sufficient to establish serious misconduct. It could result in a warning if the evidence shows less serious offending. Sometimes both parties may be disciplined if the evidence shows the complainant and respondent have behaved inappropriately.

2. Proceed to an informal intervention involving mediation or facilitation. This is a very common outcome. However, it is often far more difficult to achieve an informal resolution because of the negative effect of the investigation process. This will be necessary if the parties are to continue to work together. If the investigation does not lead to a disciplinary outcome, it will be necessary to seek resolution through an informal intervention.

The formal process sometimes results in a respondent leaving before the investigation is complete. This can protect them from having a negative report on their file. It means the organisation should not declare this information to other employers who seek references.

Sometimes the complainant may leave an organisation before the investigation process is complete. The stress involved can take its toll on people's health. Investigation processes can be very disruptive and destructive to people and to organisations.

¶7-100 Principles of natural justice

Fairness is important to any investigation process. There are 3 aspects to this:

1. The person investigating a complaint must be fair and free from bias. If the investigator has bias, this can lead to predetermined outcomes that can skew the findings. Sometimes people within organisations shouldn't investigate cases because of an inherent bias to protect the organisation or people in positions of authority. This is not a requirement legally in Australia or New Zealand. However, it is important for the investigator to be unbiased and competent enough to investigate without fear or favour.
2. The process of investigation must be fair. Interviews should be conducted without bias or predetermination. People have a right to be heard and to respond fully to allegations or counter-allegations. There should be no leading questions. People should be informed of their rights and support options. Parties should be given time to read and understand allegations before responding to them. They should be able to name relevant witnesses and have their testimony included in the investigation. All evidence should be included in the investigation. People should also be able to seek legal advice. The process of investigation should follow evidential leads that are reasonable. People should not be protected because they have positional authority or have friends in authority. The process of investigation should be transparent and documented, so that it is clear why an investigator has chosen to follow a line of enquiry.
3. The outcome of an investigation must be fair. Findings must be based on the evidence. They cannot be based on people's opinions or hearsay.

> Sometimes genuine claims of bullying and harassment are not upheld because the respondent denies the allegations and there is no other evidence to support the claim.

¶7-110 Standard of proof and evidence

It is important to have sufficient evidence before making a complaint. There is a "standard of proof" that must be established to have a complaint upheld. If there is insufficient evidence, the whole process may be a waste of time, at best, or it may make things worse for the complainant.

The standard of proof in civil courts where employment cases are heard is known as the "Balance of Probability". This means that there must be sufficient evidence that "it is more likely than not that an allegation is true". This is a lower threshold than the standard of proof in a criminal court. This standard of proof in a criminal court is known as "beyond reasonable doubt".

A strong form of evidence is witness testimony. Someone who witnessed an event where alleged bullying or harassment occurred can provide strong evidence if they are reliable and willing to be involved in an investigation.

> A complaint was made by a team member against his team leader. The complainant gave names of others in the team who had witnessed bullying incidents. The investigator interviewed those named as witnesses. However, none of them agreed to allow their testimony to be used, because they were afraid of repercussions. This meant that the allegations, having been denied by the respondent, had no other evidence to back them up. The complaint failed. The complainant resigned.

Strong evidence may also include documentary evidence such as written documents, emails, texts, social media statements or recordings. They must relate directly to the allegations and show them to be true.

People's opinions and hearsay are not evidence.

> In one workplace, the investigator asked everyone in a work team whether they thought the respondent was a bully. Based on people's comments, the investigator pronounced the complaint was unsubstantiated.

People form their opinions about others for a variety of reasons and they are subjective. An investigator might use an opinion to follow a line of enquiry, but the opinion itself is immaterial to the finding. For this reason, people who come forward to vouch for someone's good character should not be used as evidence that a person has not bullied or harassed.

> "I have known Henry for many years, and he is a good man who would not bully anyone."

This does not mean that Henry didn't bully someone during those years or that Henry did not bully someone last month. It is an opinion about a person.

Hearsay is when someone hears something about another person or situation but has not directly witnessed an event themselves. Gossip does not stand up as evidence. However, there are times when something heard second-hand can be useful to an investigator. This might lead them to interview the person who did witness the situation. If a target told someone of a bullying or harassing incident shortly after it had occurred, and this person noticed the target was distressed or upset, this could be used as evidence. It is hearsay, but there are signs of distress that have been observed:

> "She came out of the office upset and crying. When I asked her what was wrong, she said that Joe had groped her."

Other forms of evidence include circumstantial evidence such as reports from a counsellor or doctor, previous complaints between the parties, diary notes, sick leave, or absences. Circumstantial evidence are facts that can be used to infer claims.

> In a hearing, the respondent denied all allegations of bullying. The complainant produced a diary with multiple notes describing specific incidents over the year. She also produced a letter from her counsellor that described the incidents. The complainant won her case.

Another example is "similar fact evidence" (SFE). This is evidence that the respondent has bullied or harassed before. It must show more than a disposition or propensity to do something. The fact that a respondent has had a previous allegation of bullying or harassment made against them does not prove that they have bullied or harassed at a later time. Unless the type of bullying or harassment is "strikingly similar" to the current allegation, it does not meet the threshold of evidence.

> An employee who had been accused of sexual harassment in the past faced a new complaint. The complainant described the method used to groom and proposition the complainant. The method used was "strikingly similar" to the past event and was accepted as evidence in the current investigation.

It is not easy to gather evidence, especially when bullying or harassment has occurred in private without witnesses. Complainants know what happened, but proving it is difficult. An allegation that is denied by a respondent does not have standing. The denial cancels the allegation, and the onus is left to the complainant to swing the scales of justice in their favour, by providing more evidence that the allegation is true.

¶7-120 Preliminary investigations

It can be useful to start the formal investigation process with a preliminary investigation. This allows the investigator to assess the allegations and hear the responses before continuing with the full investigation process.

After preliminary discussions with the parties, it may be apparent that the alleged perpetrator is accountable, remorseful, and willing to undertake an informal process to resolve matters. If the complainant accepts this and is willing to change to an informal process, this could be beneficial to everyone involved.

After interviewing the complainant, the investigator may consider the allegations to be unlikely to be serious enough to warrant a disciplinary finding of serious misconduct, even if the allegations are substantiated. The complainant may want to reconsider continuing with the complaint or choose an informal intervention instead.

If there is one incident being complained of, the investigator might inform the complainant that the complaint will not reach the threshold of the definition of bullying. There has not been "repeated" bullying behaviour. An investigator might raise this after the initial meeting with the complainant and suggest an alternative informal intervention.

It is possible to change from a formal to an informal process if the complainant wants that. However, once a complaint has been made and the respondent has been informed, matters can quickly become adversarial.

> In one organisation, seven people complained against their team leader. The senior manager informed the team leader that seven people had made complaints, but did not provide the names or the details of the complaints. The team leader was upset because she could not refute anonymous allegations. The senior manager decided to undertake a preliminary investigation by an external investigator. The investigator met initially with the complainants to examine their allegations and asked the complainants what outcome they wanted. They explained that they didn't want the team leader to be dismissed but wanted her behaviour to change. The investigator explained that they could change their process from formal to informal and how this could be used to achieve the outcome they wanted. They agreed to change the process, and the investigator met with the team leader. She was angry at the way the process had begun and said she would be taking the matter up with external employment authorities. The investigator then informed her that the complainants had decided to withdraw their complaints in favour of an informal process if she was agreeable. The team leader considered her options and then agreed. The formal complaint was withdrawn. The outcome involved a process where matters were discussed in a group process. Agreements were made regarding future

behaviour, ongoing support and monitoring. The complainants and the team leader understood that unless the matter was resolved and behaviour changed, the complaint could be reinstated. This provided an incentive to resolve concerns at an informal level.

Preliminary investigations can be useful, but they should not be used to coerce people to withdraw complaints. Investigators should allow people to make informed choices, and sometimes they may choose to opt for different processes to resolve matters.

Employers can refuse to investigate formal complaints on the grounds that the allegations are frivolous or vexatious. There would need to be sufficient evidence to establish that. The risk is the complainant could take their complaint to an external authority.

¶7-130 Advantages and disadvantages of the formal option

The only advantage of the formal option is that an employer can take disciplinary action against an employee who has behaved inappropriately. If the offending is serious enough, or it is reasonable to conclude the offender will continue to offend, then an employer should dismiss. This requires courage and commitment from employers. However, failing to dismiss, when necessary, sends a message to the organisation that bullying and harassment will be tolerated. This can create distrust of management and of the organisation.

In cases of sexual and racial harassment, formal complaint options are often more appropriate. This is because of the nature of this harassment and the impact upon targets. It may be very difficult to restore trust after significant harassment has occurred, and the issue is more likely to be considered serious misconduct.

The disadvantages of the formal option are considerable. They are costly personally and financially, take considerable time to complete, and cause significant stress to everyone involved. The impact of a formal complaint and investigation on teams can be very difficult to recover from. It often creates long-term negative effects, polarisation, and ongoing distrust and disruption. People will be pressured to take sides and form alliances. This doesn't heal itself once the investigation has finished.

It is obvious that a formal complaint system is necessary. However, those who make formal complaints should consider the following:

- Is there sufficient evidence to support the allegation of bullying or harassment? If not, it might be better to wait until there is sufficient evidence or choose an informal process. There are no winners in a failed complaint.

- Will witnesses give their evidence? If there is a climate of fear, witnesses may not speak up, and crucial evidence will not be presented.
- Who will conduct the investigation, and are they sufficiently unbiased and competent? If not, then who else could investigate? Will the employer allow an external investigator?
- Is there a clear investigation process, and how will the parties be kept safe during the process?
- What disciplinary outcomes are likely if the investigation finds substance?
- If there is insufficient substance, what will likely happen?

Complainants should do some checking of these areas with the appropriate managers before committing to a formal complaint. They are usually unaware of the disadvantages.

These include:

- If there is insufficient evidence, the complaint will result in a finding of "insufficient substance". This could leave the complainant in a difficult position in their workplace.
- Even if there is sufficient evidence to prove bullying or harassment, this may not result in the respondent being dismissed. Summary dismissal is only an option when there is significant evidence of serious bullying and harassment. This may mean that the complainant will still have to work with the respondent.
- If there is sufficient evidence to prove bullying or harassment, the disciplinary outcome against the respondent will be kept confidential. The complainant has a right to know the findings of an investigation but not the subsequent disciplinary outcomes. This is a private matter between the employer and the respondent. Many complainants are left unaware of any consequences for the respondent.
- If the finding of an investigation proves that the complainant has acted inappropriately, the complainant may be subject to disciplinary action. Acting inappropriately includes reciprocal bullying and other forms of misconduct.
- If the complainant makes false and reckless allegations, this may lead to the complainant being dismissed. Note: false allegations are different from findings of insufficient evidence.

¶7-140 Advantages and disadvantages of the informal intervention option

The main advantage of the informal option is that it provides a way for people to resolve matters reasonably quickly and effectively. Rather than being an adversarial dynamic, informal interventions provide an opportunity for people to learn how to work together more cooperatively. The fact that informal processes do not begin with allegations being put in writing creates a different kind of response. Informal interventions can be undertaken without much disruption to the workplace. Staff are less likely to leave after informal interventions, and people often value and appreciate the outcomes as beneficial to all concerned.

The main disadvantage of the informal option is that it requires some skills and competence by managers who conduct it. Managers who naively call people to a meeting to "sort things out" may find that the situation explodes into a fight or a walk-out. Care must be taken, and managers need to understand different ways to engage without prematurely bringing people together for face-to-face meetings. They also need to know how to facilitate a face-to-face meeting to avoid it becoming unmanageable.

The other main disadvantage of the informal option is that it may not prevent further bullying or harassment. Some people will not change their behaviour, and this is more likely with sexual harassment. Sometimes there is a temporary change for a week or so, and then the perpetrator reverts to old patterns of behaviour. This will create further disruption and may require further informal interventions. The situation may require a subsequent formal complaint. Informal interventions do not carry any guarantee of success.

There is actually no guarantee of success under any of the 3 options. Targets should think through their options carefully and get information before they decide what to do.

¶7-150 Differences between informal and formal options

Informal	Formal
Concerns are raised	A complaint is made
Cooperative dynamics (win/win)	Adversarial dynamics (win/lose)
Exploration process	Investigation process
Non-disciplinary	Potential disciplinary outcomes
Creative and varied processes	Rigid investigation process
Person who initiates (concerned person) maintains high degree of control of process and outcomes	Complainant has no control of process and outcome; process and outcomes decided by management
Emphasis on verbal communication between parties	Emphasis on written communication between parties

Informal	Formal
Allegations are not kept on a person's file; only the agreement made between the parties is kept on file	All material is kept on file
Focus on the relationship between people	Focus on justice and assigning blame
Long-term results	Short-term results
Quick and inexpensive	Longer and more expensive

Organisations sometimes make the mistake of mixing informal and formal processes. This is usually problematic.

- A person raises concerns about bullying and harassment (informal) but is then asked to put allegations in writing (formal).
- A person submits a written formal complaint (formal) and is told the organisation will arrange a mediation (informal).
- A person agrees to mediation (informal) and wants the allegations to be put into writing because their lawyer has requested this (formal).
- A person agrees to mediation (informal) but requests their lawyer attend as their representative in their absence (formal).

It is very common for people to become adversarial whenever issues are raised with them. This appears to be more common at senior levels in organisations. In risk-averse and conflict-avoidant workplace cultures people veer toward formal processes rather than informal ones. They go to war, fighting and defending. This creates even more risk for organisations.

The fear of conflict creates a dangerous environment overall. Organisations need to make conflict resolution the norm and provide processes to do this. Conflict is then seen as an opportunity for growth and improvement.

We need informal and formal options. Both are important and have their place. We need these processes to be kept separate and distinct from each other. Targets should not have to go through an informal process before initiating a formal complaint. There are times when going straight to a formal complaint is the most appropriate thing to do, especially with sexual and racial harassment.

Chapter 8

Case Study: How Things Can Go Badly Wrong

¶8-010 Case study

In a team of 25, 2 men became embroiled in a conflict over the allocation of work resources. The older man on 4 separate occasions used threatening behaviour towards the younger man. This included yelling, displays of anger, swearing, invasion of personal space and verbal threats. In addition to this, the older man refused to communicate and ignored the younger man during normal daily interactions. This increased the level of passive hostility and disrupted communication between them. The younger man did not use bullying behaviour in response, although he argued his point of view during confrontations with the older man. The younger man became distressed because of the breakdown in the relationship. He respected the older man's skills and experience and didn't want things to get worse. He tried on 2 occasions to talk through things with the older man, in the hope of resolving matters, but this didn't work.

The younger man spoke with the manager of the team. The manager listened and expressed concern but did nothing. The younger man approached the manager again and was then asked to put his concerns in writing. The young man went home and drafted a summary of what had happened, how he was affected, and his thoughts about the situation. He gave the document to his manager the next day.

The manager forwarded the document to the human resources (HR) manager. The HR manager started an investigation under the company's bullying and harassment policy.

The older man received the complaint and was told that the company would investigate. They requested that the older man be suspended from the workplace while the investigation proceeded. The older man took leave with pay and the investigation process began. The HR manager interviewed both men individually, as well as others named as witnesses to incidents.

After 2 months, the investigation process was completed. The older man was found guilty of bullying the younger man. The matter moved to a disciplinary process, and the older man received a written warning. An external facilitator was then employed to provide a mediation between the 2 men, prior to the older man returning to work.

The facilitator met with both men and with the manager separately. The older man appeared anxious and depressed, because he had been on leave facing uncertainty about his job. He was also upset that the younger man had made a formal complaint about him. They had previously been friends, and this kind of action had not been taken before in the history of the team.

The younger man appeared anxious and depressed when the facilitator met with him. He was being targeted by half the team, who thought his actions were wrong. Another group sided with the young man. The team was divided into 2 camps. The younger man was confused because he didn't understand how it had come to this. He had wanted help and support from his manager, not the investigation process that had occurred.

The facilitator spoke with the manager and asked why he had chosen to request a written account from the younger man. The manager believed his actions were reasonable because the company had a zero-tolerance policy, which stated that all bullying and harassment should be reported. When the facilitator informed the manager that the young man had simply wanted help to resolve the situation, the manager said he was acting on advice from human resources.

A mediation was conducted, and the parties agreed to a return-to-work process. They were both concerned that others in the team would seek to stir matters up. Tensions within the group had risen significantly, with people taking sides for and against the 2 men. Some who had made statements as witnesses were also reportedly being targeted by others. The team had become divided and there was significant confusion and gossip being spread. The relationship between the manager and the team overall had deteriorated. The manager faced considerable anger and resentment from people within the team. Both men were angry at the actions of the manager. Others expressed a lack of confidence in the manager. The younger man took sick leave after the mediation and later resigned from the workplace.

¶8-020 Reflections

This is an example of what unfortunately occurs in many workplaces when someone raises concerns about bullying or harassment. They are told to put their concerns in writing and report it. The matter turns into an investigation process and has a significant destructive impact that may be very difficult to resolve.

It is useful to reflect on what happened in this story. Let's consider alternatives.

Was this an effective way to deal with the situation? Did it produce a good result?

- The complainant resigned after a lengthy absence on paid sick leave.
- The respondent was off work for two months on paid leave.

- The team became polarised over what had happened.
- The manager became less confident in his ability to manage.
- The team manager and HR became distrusted and rejected by the team overall.
- The financial costs relating to disruption, disengagement, sick leave, external facilitation, lost work time, and resignation were significant.
- One person received a written warning.

This story involves bullying behaviour between 2 peers in a workplace, despite one man being older than the other. It is a case of horizontal bullying, not vertical bullying. The 2 men had been friends, although their relationship had deteriorated over work conflicts. One man had resorted to bullying behaviour against the other. It was not reciprocal. The other man had become increasingly distressed over the situation.

None of the team, including the manager, had received any significant training on preventing bullying and harassment. They lacked understanding of how bullying is defined or what might be examples of bullying. Although the company had developed an anti-bullying and harassment policy, they had not provided any significant education about the policy. The manager had received limited information. The policy itself had shortcomings. It emphasised a zero-tolerance approach. It stated that all instances of bullying or harassment should be reported. Although it mentioned informal processes like mediation to resolve matters of bullying and harassment, its requirement for people to report all incidents created a problem. The policy led the manager to ask the younger man to put his claims in writing.

Both men had strong relationships within the team. The resourcing issues had been long-term and involved some complicated aspects. It affected several people and caused frustration among the team. There was a degree of polarisation with some team members over the resourcing issue. Some people supported the older man's position, and others supported the younger man's position.

The 4 bullying incidents had been witnessed by others, and no one had intervened. This is an important factor, because it shows there was a high level of passive collusion in the team. Among team members, there were different views about the reasonableness of the older man's behaviour. They blamed the resourcing issue itself for what had happened. There was an "us and them" dynamic already in the team prior to the investigation. This aspect of team dynamics became worse during the investigation process. Within the team, there was also a high tolerance for displays of anger and verbal abuse. Some people had concerns about the level of anger displayed and yet did not speak up or challenge it. There was a significant shadow in this team.

The 2 men had previously related well with the manager, but both considered he was conflict-avoidant.

The manager considered the team dynamics to be difficult at times. He struggled with some people in the team and found it difficult to assert his authority. He avoided conflict because he lacked confidence and didn't know what to do in some situations. He resorted to anger himself over some issues, and this reinforced the belief that displays of anger were acceptable.

This environment is one where bullying and harassment thrive. People don't speak up, there is a lack of knowledge about the dynamics of bullying and harassment, and there is a high level of acceptance of these destructive behaviours. Within the team, there are divisions and alliances. Complaining about bullying or harassment has never occurred before in this team. Complaining formally is frowned upon because it involves senior management, who are considered to be outside of the group.

Some dominant beliefs within the team include:

- People should harden up and put up with bad behaviour.
- People should stand up for themselves and sort things out themselves.
- People who are not hard enough are weak and should leave.
- People should not "snitch on" or "dob in" their fellow workers.
- Aggression and belligerence are strengths.
- Those in authority don't know what they are doing most of the time and their involvement is not welcome.

In a social and cultural environment where these beliefs and norms are present, bullying will become accepted and protected by silence and collusion. People do not speak up because of fear of reprisal. Complaints are not made. People who are hurt by bullying or harassment leave, and this reinforces the social system that exists.

¶8-030 Alternative approaches

The most efficient way to prevent bullying and harassment in any team involves the team itself. When a team is healthy, there is a level of shared concern and care about all the members. If one is picked on, then others stand up and challenge this. In this way healthy teams regulate their own behaviour.

When the older man displayed bullying behaviour, those who witnessed it could have intervened. The young man could have spoken up directly to the older man and had support from the team to do so. However, this was unlikely to happen because the dominant beliefs of the group prevented it.

Education on bullying and harassment could have initiated some changes in the team. However, it is unlikely that a single training course would have made a long-term difference.

In addition, the manager could have been more "hands on" by resolving issues before they became serious. The manager could have modelled different behaviour that would not reinforce anger as a way of resolving problems. The team could have developed more competence in working through issues cooperatively and taking responsibility for the dynamics of the team.

Teams that have high levels of trust, cohesion and mutuality behave differently than this team. There is a greater level of care and mutual support. Team development could have created change but would have required time.

The zero-tolerance policy was simplistic and needed to be upgraded to emphasise informal intervention processes. Education about this could have led to other outcomes.

The manager could have asked the younger man what outcome he wanted, and this would probably have led to an informal intervention. An effective process could have involved the manager approaching the older man to discuss what was going on between himself and the younger man. This would have led to a discussion about the resourcing issues as well. He could have initiated a conversation that covered the following areas:

- the issues from the older man's perspective
- the issues from the younger man's perspective
- the issues from the manager's perspective, including the need to prevent bullying.

This approach would have involved the manager going between the 2 men and devising some agreements that would resolve the issues at stake.

To do this, the manager would have needed to get permission from the younger man to speak about his concerns with the older man. The manager could have said something like:

> "I will approach (older man) and let him know that you have approached me with some concerns about the situation between you. This will probably lead to a discussion about the resources issue, but I will also discuss behaviour and how this issue is being addressed. I will let him know that you have concerns about the level of aggression and anger being used. I will hear his version of things and then I will let you know how that conversation went."

The manager, by intervening this way, could have explored the issues from both perspectives, set some expectations around future behaviour, and resolved what had been happening.

Because the informal intervention is not a formal complaint, nothing is put in writing. People often feel a greater level of threat when they read comments on paper, rather than receiving verbal information. They are more likely to become adversarial and defensive.

When the manager approached the older man, he would have needed to be careful not to make hasty judgments until he had heard the older man's perspective. He would have needed to take on a role of a respectful enquirer before moving into the role of solution finder.

Language is important. It is best to come across in a way that doesn't inflame the situation by using highly charged language. Imagine how different these 2 approaches might be and what they might provoke in response:

> "How are things going between you and (younger man)?"
>
> "Why are you asking that?"
>
> "He approached me and expressed some concerns about how things are between you. I have suggested that I come and have a chat with you about this."

This approach could be described as respectfully curious. It invites an open response. It isn't loaded with emotive content or blaming. He could have described things as tense or strained but it is often unnecessary to describe things beyond "how things are between you".

In contrast, the manager could have invited a more defensive approach by starting with:

> "What's going on between you and (younger man)?"
>
> "Why are you asking that?"
>
> "He has complained that you are bullying him."

This approach invites quite a different response, simply because of language. This approach would probably trigger a more defensive response. The use of words such as "complained" and "bullying" are highly charged words. It would increase the tension, and people often don't react well when they are tense. Language is important, but so is the overall approach.

After approaching the older man and letting him know about the younger man's concerns, the manager might have got a different perspective on matters. After hearing this, he would then have needed to consider the most effective process to resolve things.

He might have heard concerns from the older man about the younger man's behaviour. He would probably have heard about the older man's views of the resources issue. The manager would have needed to remain objective and consider a suitable course of action.

Remaining neutral and empathetic allows people to find more effective solutions. Sympathy is feeling sorry for someone, and it is not very helpful in these situations. If the manager is sympathetic, he will have heard the younger man's version and felt sorry for him, which would possibly have clouded his judgment. When talking with the older man, this would have come through in his communication. By being empathetic, the manager would have gained an understanding of the concerns and needs of the younger man but remained open to understanding the concerns and needs of the older man as well.

Imagine that the manager listens to the older man and hears that he is frustrated because of the resourcing issue. The older man is also frustrated with the younger man's behaviour, because the younger man doesn't communicate with the older man when he takes action to get his resources. This action by the younger man, without consultation, affects the older man.

The manager might now have 2 perspectives and 2 sets of needs to consider:

Younger man's concerns/needs	Older man's concerns/needs
• Displays of anger and aggression • Lack of open communication from older man • Safety needs • Communication needs	• Resource process • Lack of communication from younger man • Fairness needs • Communication needs

There is a third perspective to consider. It is the needs of the employer. The employer has a bullying and harassment prevention policy that needs to be upheld. The manager needs to provide guidance to both men to reduce the likelihood of further acts of aggression.

The manager is working toward a resolution. He has the trust of both parties and he needs to relay the needs and concerns of both parties to each other. In the conversation with the older man, he could summarise and say:

> "I can see that you are frustrated because (younger man) doesn't inform you when he accesses resources that you also need. You want him to talk with you, and that is fair enough, but he is also concerned about what happens when he does talk to you. He says you get angry and aggressive. That concerns him. So, part of this is about how you both communicate with each other. I also have an obligation under health and safety to ensure people feel safe at work and are not exposed to unacceptable behaviour such as bullying, and this could be seen as bullying. I want some commitment about toning things down from here on."
>
> "OK. If he will communicate with me, then I will turn the anger down."

There is a principle involved in this kind of resolution process. It is that people often become far more conciliatory when they believe their concerns have been heard and attended to. While the parties may have lost trust in each other, they can form trust in the manager who attends to their separate needs fairly. Trust then can develop between the parties.

The manager returns to the younger man and explains the older man's perspective but also relays the older man's willingness to agree to a resolution. The manager presses both parties to a workable solution, and this solution could be outlined in a written document that can be used to guide the parties in the future.

Resolution processes have 2 parts. The first part is the specific agreements of the parties. This involves verbal or written commitments. The second part is reconnection of the parties.

If the manager were to write up an agreement between the parties, it might look like this:

> Agreement between (younger man) and (older man) and Team Manager (date)
>
> The parties agree to the following:
>
> 1. to review the process of allocating resources and hear from the rest of the team (manager action item)
> 2. to inform each other of resourcing needs before initiating claims to resources
> 3. to communicate respectfully with each other
> 4. to refrain from displays of anger or other potentially threatening behaviour
> 5. to continue showing mutual support toward each other.

The second part of the resolution process involves the reconnection of the parties. Sometimes this is referred to as closure because it completes the process. While the manager has spoken to both parties, they have not spoken to each other. Without something being said, they may continue to hold resentment toward each other.

Closure is usually achieved by people communicating directly with each other. This can involve:

- acknowledgements about past behaviour and its impact
- thanking the other person for choosing to resolve matters
- verbal commitments to agreements
- expressions of hope.

Closure is important because without it people will often continue to ignore each other or hold resentment. Apologies are not necessary for closure and should never be demanded. What is important is acknowledgement and commitment.

Imagine how differently this informal intervention might have been from the formal process that did occur.

While some may argue that informal approaches do not achieve any justice for complainants, they achieve resolution of issues and improved relationships instead. Is justice the most important goal?

Chapter 9

How to Engage with Someone Who Raises Concerns

¶9-010 How to respond to concerns

Most people who experience bullying or harassment want to talk with someone about it. If an organisation has trained contact persons, they can provide a confidential "first point of contact" service. This can help resolve issues at a low level. Early intervention is crucial, and because contact persons are trusted peers, they are accessible to people.

People may also approach managers. If the concerns are about a peer in a work team, it is likely that the first-level supervisor will be the one who is approached. If the supervisor is the subject of concern, the concerned person may approach the manager above the supervisor. People usually approach someone they know who will listen to them.

It is therefore important that supervisors and managers understand how to respond when a person raises concerns. They need to know what to do and what not to do, because this is a crucial stage and mistakes can be costly. Some common mistakes managers make are:

- making faulty assumptions and conclusions
- downplaying concerns and minimising risks
- blaming the target
- lacking empathy
- sympathetic responses that reinforce victimhood and helplessness
- defensiveness
- patronising responses
- making empty promises that the issue will be "looked into" and then doing nothing
- starting an impromptu investigation that is not fair or unbiased
- telling the person their concerns are unfounded
- pushing a person into mediation
- requesting that concerns be put in writing.

Information from the 0800 ZEROBULLY helpline found that 72% of callers who had reported concerns about bullying or harassment to management were disappointed with the way managers responded. Moreover, 53% said that raising concerns resulted in matters becoming worse for them. They were viewed as troublemakers or blamed for the situation.

¶9-020 The EXPLORE Model

The EXPLORE model developed by WAVE provides a guide for that initial conversation with a concerned person. It covers points in the conversation process that a manger can use to gain critical information and provide effective responses. It also explores the options for resolution and ends with the development of a shared plan. This model should be used in a flexible way. Not all conversations start in the same way or move through a linear process. The model gives key pointers that can assist a manager to have a productive and empowering conversation.

The EXPLORE Model

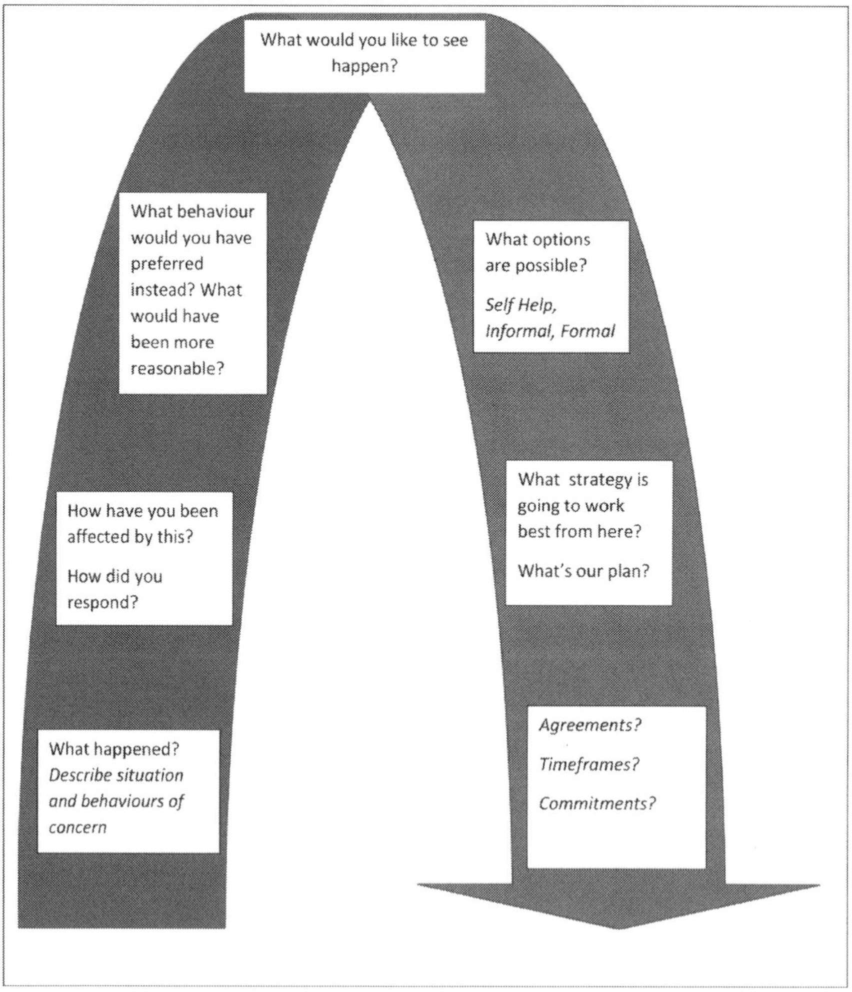

The EXPLORE Model begins on one side of the curve, exploring what has happened and the effects of what has happened. It also assists the enquirer to consider their responses and, most importantly, what would have been a preferred or more reasonable action by the person they are concerned about.

At the apex of the curve is the point of turning and a question that is often very empowering. It allows the concerned person to think about what they want. This provides a basis for the next level: the exploration of options and the creation of a plan.

A manager who uses the EXPLORE model assists the enquirer to:

- reflect on their concerns
- increase their own self-awareness
- understand their specific needs and emotional responses
- focus on what is primarily important to them
- develop empathy for the person they are concerned about
- explore self-help, informal and formal options
- consider possible advantages and disadvantages
- develop a shared plan.

The manager who uses the EXPLORE model should have key guiding principles.

¶9-030 Guiding principles

- **Non-judgmental listening.** This means putting aside personal bias and judgments that can create distortion of information. When we have a bias, we begin to see with blinkers on. We see and hear what confirms our bias and we don't see and hear what is contrary to our bias. This is called the confirmation bias.
- **Objectivity.** This involves realising that you are hearing a story from one person's perspective and standing back from making early judgments. There will be other perspectives. This is normal. Managers should be wary of making assumptions.
- **Empathy rather than sympathy.** It is possible to listen and empathise without being sympathetic and agreeing with one person's judgments and perceptions. Empathy is shown by expressing an understanding of a person's experience. Seek to understand what the person is grappling with and what is important to them. Seek to understand their values and their fears. Don't try and soothe them with sympathy.
- **Active listening.** This involves reflection of content and emotions, paraphrasing and summarising. Ask open questions without sounding like an interrogator. These basic listening skills assist a manager to gain a

deeper understanding. They also provide the enquirer with the opportunity to reflect on their experiences, goals and motivations.

Let's address each aspect of the model in more detail:

1. What's been happening?

People often start talking about bullying and harassment in a generalised and personalised way. It is important to focus the conversation on specific situations that have occurred.

> Enquirer: "There is a lot of bullying happening in this team." (generalisation)
>
> Manager: "What sort of things are happening?" (specifics)
>
> Enquirer: "The team leader is a bully." (personalisation)
>
> Manager: "You sound concerned about what is happening. I would like to get a clearer picture of the sorts of things that have occurred. Can you tell me about the kind of bullying you are referring to and the situations you have witnessed?"

Don't assume that because someone says they are being bullied they are. They may be angry about not getting their own way over an issue. Get down to specifics. People are often afraid to speak up, or they may be disturbed by what they have experienced. It can be helpful for a manager to acknowledge the emotions present or acknowledge the motivation of the person.

> "You sound concerned and you want to see something done about it. Help me understand exactly what has happened."

Sometimes it can be useful to talk about the most recent incident that has occurred. At other times it can be useful to talk about the first incident. The most important thing is to gain a detailed account of the kinds of behaviours that have occurred:

> "What happened next?"
>
> "What did they say?"
>
> "What did they do?"
>
> "How did you respond?"

These open questions allow a person to describe things in detail, rather than just expressing an opinion about what happened.

The manager should focus on 2 main aspects:

- facts about the situation and how it occurred
- the behaviour involved and whether it was reasonable or not.

It is also important that a manager is careful when asking questions, so the conversation doesn't resemble an interrogation process. It is important to paraphrase and summarise during the conversation to ensure that the manager has understood things. It is also useful for the enquirer to hear back what they have said:

> Manager: "Let me see if I have got this right. You are saying that the team leader said. . . and did . . ."
>
> Enquirer: "Yes, and there was also another thing that I forgot to mention."

2. How did this affect you?

It is important to understand how someone has been affected by the situations they have experienced and to talk about the impact of incidents. This is more than simply asking, "How did this make you feel?" Sometimes it is very apparent what a person felt, and it can be more useful to name it.

> "It sounds as if you were shocked by that?"

People are affected in a variety of ways when they experience bullying or harassment. It can affect a person emotionally, cognitively and physically.

Some useful questions to explore are:

> "How did you feel when that happened?"
>
> "What were you thinking when that happened?"
>
> "What was happening physically to you, in your body, while this was happening?"

In addition, effects can be short term and long term:

> "Initially I felt shocked by what she said to me. Afterwards I felt anxious about what might come after this. It reminded me of another time when I was bullied as a child. I didn't realise how much it had affected me. Now I find myself feeling angry about it and I have been thinking of leaving."

Effects can also include how their work has been affected. It is important to allow some time to explore the effects in a non-judgmental way.

¶9-040 Primary and secondary emotions

People may approach a manager with strong feelings. It is common for anger to be expressed, and sometimes people cry, tremble with fear, freeze up with shock, express confusion or anxiety, or even express shame or guilt. Emotions are important and should not be avoided or discouraged. Emotions reveal what is happening on the inside. They are not wrong. They are very real indicators to understand deeper core needs.

One way of understanding emotions is to recognise that there are primary and secondary emotions.

Primary emotions are instantaneous emotions directly associated with a person's core needs. For example, when a person is threatened, they will probably experience fear. Their need for safety and security has been violated.

Primary emotions include fear, sadness, hurt, shock and feeling overwhelmed. Fear is probably the most common, with its subsidiary feelings of panic, anxiety or terror. When someone is bullied or harassed, they may experience a range of these primary emotions. This is completely normal and natural.

It is important not to try to resolve the feelings or minimise them. Instead, acknowledge them.

Secondary emotions arise after primary emotions. Fear can quickly turn to anger, which is the secondary emotion. Sadness can turn to despair. Secondary emotions are created after the person makes internal judgments about what has happened, and this creates a different feeling. Secondary emotions can be a way of replacing the primary feelings.

> Enquirer: "How dare he speak to me like that. Who does he think he is?" (anger)
>
> "I couldn't believe what I was hearing and seeing?" (shock)
>
> Manager: "What else were you feeling under all of that?"
>
> Enquirer: "I was hurt by what he said, and as I think about it now I feel sad that I no longer am able to trust him." (primary emotions of hurt and grief)

By focusing on the anger and shock, the manager will encourage more of these secondary emotions. If you only deal with the secondary emotions, do not be surprised if the person decides to do something that exacerbates and inflames things, such as fighting back or seeking vengeance. Focusing on secondary emotions tends to keep people stuck in those secondary emotions. Focusing on primary emotions allows people to access their deeper needs. This is important to resolve those feelings.

> Enquirer: "How dare he speak to me like that. Who does he think he is?" (anger)
>
> "I couldn't believe what I was hearing and seeing?" (shock)
>
> Manager: "That's terrible."

The problem with secondary emotions is that they can lead people into areas that later they might regret. They do not relate to their core needs, and therefore they can create outcomes that are unwanted in the long term. Primary emotions relate to core needs.

> Enquirer: "I am angry about what has happened."
>
> Manager: "Were you initially angry when the incident occurred?"

Enquirer: "No. I think I was more afraid to say anything when it happened."

Manager: "So at first you felt afraid and then the anger came later."

Enquirer: "Yes. I thought her tantrum was childish."

Manager: "What specifically were you feeling afraid of when the tantrum occurred?"

Enquirer: "I think mostly I was afraid of being overwhelmed, and I couldn't think of anything to say in the moment. I was unable to stand up to her. I felt weak and powerless."

". . . as I say this, I feel ashamed of how weak I am." (secondary emotion of shame)

Manager: "So you want to be able to stand up to her and not be overwhelmed."

Enquirer: "Yeah. I wish I could have stood my ground with her."

Why is the understanding about primary and secondary emotions useful? It is useful because the enquirer can learn something about themselves and their core needs. It increases self-awareness and may assist them to make effective choices about what to do.

In the case above, the core area of need is to feel a sense of stability and power in the face of another person's anger. The enquirer wants an alternative to fear. They want to sustain themselves and have more agency, which will help them to feel more secure and act with confidence.

If the manager were to focus on the anger and the judgments the enquirer made, this would increase the enquirer's experience of anger and judgment. This might lead to a completely different set of outcomes.

Manager: "You sound angry that she threw a childish tantrum."

Enquirer: "It's pathetic really. If that's how she is going to treat me, then I will make a complaint."

Manager: "She is a bully."

It is important that a manager responds with empathy rather than sympathy. Sympathy leads to agreeing with the person's judgments, and this can be dangerous. Empathy allows the person to understand themselves and their core needs, then make choices that will serve those needs.

Unfortunately, many people who experience bullying and harassment make decisions to fight back and get justice because they are full of anger and self-righteous indignation. They make formal complaints, take personal grievances, bully back, and fight it out. They want to be right and make the other wrong. They want the person punished. They want to win. Unfortunately, they usually lose.

It is not wrong to make formal complaints or take personal grievances. There is a time and a place for doing that. However, the issue is, what emotional place is motivating the action and what needs are being met? The desire to win might not be in the person's best interests.

> In a university, a professor alleged she was bullied, and she made a complaint. Because it was only one incident, the complaint failed to meet the threshold of bullying (there were no repeated behaviours within the range). The professor then faced a counter-complaint regarding her work. This wasn't substantiated. However, the person who bullied then began to spread rumours and to undermine the work of the professor. This created a polarising effect among staff, and the professor continued to fight back. She took a personal grievance with the Employment Relations Authority. She now faced the university's lawyers and was unable to win her case after mediation and a court hearing. After 18 months, her health began to deteriorate. She finally left the university, diagnosed with an anxiety disorder and depression. When asked about her ordeal, she said she wished she had left earlier: "I am a fighter. I didn't want them to win, and I was not going to lose. But they have won, and I am no longer employable, so I have lost. I have lost everything."

Unfortunately, many people are quick to fight and slow to learn that going to war is costly. Once a person starts down the path of fighting it out, it is difficult to reverse and seek other forms of resolution.

> "An eye for an eye, and a tooth for a tooth ensures everyone becomes blind and toothless."

3. What would you have preferred instead?

This line of enquiry is useful to explore. It allows the person to imagine a more reasonable way the perpetrator could have behaved. It invites them to think about a preferred situation.

It also allows the person to think about what might have been motivating the person to do what they did. This is creative and empowering because it considers the other person's needs and motivations.

> Manager: "You have said that he became angry and stood over you. He accused you of wasting his time and made some threats about your future here. At first you were stunned and didn't know what to say. He then walked out, slamming the door."
>
> Enquirer: "He really was angry with me, but I hadn't been briefed on what he wanted. He assumes I know what he wants and doesn't check that I understand what he wants."
>
> Manager: "So the anger might be related to not getting the results he wanted?"

Enquirer: "Pretty much. He's under pressure, I guess, but that doesn't make it OK."

Manager: "How could he have done this better? What would you have preferred instead of what you got?"

Enquirer: "He could have approached me without the anger, and he could have asked beforehand if I knew what to do. That would have been better. He could have asked some questions in a calm way."

The benefit of leading the discussion into this area is that it enables the enquirer to empathise with the other person and to consider their experience. It is also useful because the enquirer has a chance to create a better alternative. This employs creative thinking and solution finding. Rather than being a helpless victim, the enquirer is accessing their own creative functioning and making assessments. Even if incorrect, the reality of seeking to empathise and understand the other person is useful.

4. The empowering question: What would you like to see happen?

At the apex of the EXPLORE model is the empowering question. This allows the enquirer to think ahead about the best possible outcome for themselves. It is empowering because it centres on the enquirer and what this person wants, instead of what the manager thinks is best. It is sometimes best to bring this question up after summarising what has gone before:

Manager: "You have talked about an incident where your team leader became angry with you, stood over, you and made some threatening statements toward you. Initially you were shocked, and you felt unable to stand up for yourself as you would have liked. He walked out slamming the door before you had much time to compose yourself. Later you have felt angry about the situation."

Enquirer: "That's about the sum of it."

Manager: "I want you to think about what you want to see happen from here. What sort of outcome do you want out of this?"

People often pause with this question and think deeply about what is important to them. It is often useful to wait and not jump in with suggestions.

Typically, people say something like: "I just want this kind of thing to stop."

This is a common expression and a useful one.

Sometimes, they might say: "I want this person dismissed."

If this is the outcome they want, then the only way for that to happen would be to win a complaint of serious misconduct. However, if the person wants a change of behaviour, then other options could be appropriate.

Sometimes a person will find it difficult to answer this question, because it means they need to imagine a different kind of situation. It may take some time to imagine what they really want:

> Enquirer: "I don't want to experience this kind of thing again. I want him to communicate better, of course. But I doubt he can change, so I guess maybe I should find another job."

> Manager: "Well, let's explore some options other than your resignation, and you can let me know what sounds the best out of all the options. You described a preferred situation where he didn't express anger and he communicated better with you. That sounds like an outcome that could work if he is prepared to do it. You also mentioned that you wanted to be able to stand your ground with him, and that is also an important goal. Let's look at ways these goals could be met."

5. Exploring options

The 3 main options outlined in Chapter 7 are the self-help option, the informal intervention and the formal complaint. A manager should be able to discuss these options and understand the advantages and disadvantages of each.

> Manager: "Let's look at the three options. The formal complaint option is probably the most serious and would involve you making a written complaint. An investigation would then occur. However, one problem with making a formal complaint of bullying is that there has only been one incident. There needs to be more than one incident for that option to be successful. You would also need evidence to back up your complaint. At best, your complaint would serve as a warning that this sort of behaviour is unacceptable. The danger is that it could damage your relationship further and leave you with fewer options.

> Enquirer: "I don't want to go down that route."

> Manager: "Another option is that you request a conversation with him. Tell him that you were disturbed by his anger and that you want him to communicate better. I can coach you on how to have that conversation, or I can get someone else to coach you who has more expertise."

> Enquirer: "That sounds like a better idea, but I already feel a bit anxious even thinking about it."

> Manager: "Another option is that I talk with him and let him know you have raised this concern with me and that you want the issue to be resolved. I would need to hear his responses and then I could come back to you with how that went."

> Enquirer: "I think maybe at this stage it's best if I talk with him. If you get involved, it might seem as if I'm telling tales."

There is no right option when it comes to resolving issues like this. The important thing is that the enquirer can explore options without pressure. Dangers normally occur when the manager decides on the best outcome and forges ahead trying to drag the enquirer along.

6. Creating a plan

The next stage is to create a plan with the enquirer to provide a clear path forward.

A plan could be:

> Manager: "If you want to think about it overnight, I can give you a copy of the policy. I can also suggest some other material that might help you decide what you want to do. I can also check with HR about support and assistance for you. I will maintain confidentiality. Whatever happens, your safety is important, and I will support you."
>
> Enquirer: "OK, that sounds good for now. Thanks."

Plans could include:

- asking the enquirer to make notes of incidents in case they want to make a formal complaint later
- developing specific safety measures for the enquirer
- getting counselling or coaching arranged for the enquirer
- getting further advice
- considering who might be able to assist using informal interventions.

It is important that whatever plan is agreed on the enquirer is fully committed to that plan. When plans are made hastily, this can create further problems if the enquirer changes their minds or does things that undermine the plan.

Chapter 10

More on Informal Interventions

¶10-010 Informal interventions

Informal interventions are processes designed to resolve issues that arise between people. They can be useful in resolving conflicts and can be used in many cases where bullying or harassment has occurred. These processes can be simple and quick or can involve more complex interventions that require more intensive efforts over time. However, the aim of an informal intervention is resolution, stopping further bullying or harassment, and the restoration of the relationship through the development of trust and cooperation.

Successful interventions typically move through different phases:

- an exploration phase where concerns are heard
- a creative phase where resolution possibilities are examined
- an agreement phase where specific commitments are made
- a monitoring phase where supports are used to ensure the agreements and commitments are maintained.

Informal interventions work when the parties involved genuinely want matters resolved. They do not work if any party wants revenge, retribution, or punishment. If one person wants the other person to be dismissed or removed, then informal interventions will not achieve this goal and should not be used.

Informal interventions are not always appropriate, especially when significant damage has been done or the seriousness of the offences committed warrant formal proceedings. For example, in cases where there has been serious sexual harassment, the possibility of restoring trust may be unlikely. Formal processes will be more appropriate.

It is important that informal interventions happen as early as possible. People are more likely to seek an informal resolution in the early stages of a bullying or harassment experience. This is because people want it to stop:

> Manager: "You have talked about what has happened up to now and how that has affected you. What would you like to see happen from here?"
>
> Target: "I just want this behaviour to stop. I want to be able to come to work and do my job without this kind of thing continuing."

Unfortunately, the longer a person has been bullied or harassed, the less likely it is that an informal intervention process will achieve a satisfactory resolution. People become too exhausted, stressed, and polarised. They shift from wanting to sort things out and move on to fighting for justice:

> Target: "I'm not interested in sitting down and talking with this person. Why should I help them try to learn something and sort things out? I want accountability and I want them to be punished. I want an investigation."
>
> Manager: "That's your choice. If you are wanting to go through that, you will need to consider what evidence you have and you might want to get some legal advice."

Therefore, it is important that informal interventions happen at an early stage and that they happen quickly. It is also important that the most appropriate form of informal intervention is used. There is no point conducting a mediation if the parties are not ready to meet because they are afraid or angry. It is also important that the people who need to be involved are involved. Sometimes a group process is necessary because there is a need for resolution between more people.

¶10-020 Resolution

Although resolution can be achieved by a formal investigation, this is not the same kind of resolution that is sought through an informal intervention. Formal process resolutions involve decisions that are made by investigators, who determine whether complaints have substance or not. A formal resolution involves a finding and then a consequence to that, whether it is disciplinary or not. Unfortunately, many people seem to be dissatisfied with formal resolutions. They do not necessarily determine the truth. They often do not satisfy the complainant's hope for discipline or dismissal.

An informal resolution has an outcome that aims to restore relationships so that people can cooperate more effectively. Informal resolutions are restorative and remedial in that they focus on repairing damage and rebuilding.

Courts in New Zealand and Australia now include restorative justice processes because they are effective in helping people heal after being impacted by crimes. They also assist the offender to come to terms with what they have done and make needed changes.

When there is a breakdown of relationships in workplaces, restorative processes allow people to get back into a relationship with each other and move on in a productive way.

In the past, managers have often tried enforcing apologies as a way of restoring relationships. An apology would be given and sometimes this would be written. The onus would then be on the offended person to accept the apology, and this would be seen as the end of it. This sometimes doesn't work for cases of bullying or harassment, because apologies are usually done poorly. People who have been hurt often don't feel acknowledged and can't move on. When they refuse to accept a poor apology, they are viewed as the problem. However, actions rather than words are needed, and if words don't line up with actions, then the whole process is futile.

¶10-030 Problems with apologies

Apologies are often problematic, especially when they are demanded as a form of resolution. This is because an apology is an admission of guilt or wrongdoing. It is a way of confessing: "I was wrong." It is a way of seeking retribution by humiliation.

Some people do not think what they did was wrong. Things are usually more complex than being a matter of right and wrong.

In addition to this, some people simply will not apologise. It's not something they ever do. They have never learned how to apologise in a full and meaningful way. Forcing them to do so will only produce a fake apology, which can be worse than no apology.

A problem with apologies is that they are associated with adversarial systems. Sometimes an apology can be powerful if done well. Spontaneous apologies can work well, but when an apology just means saying "sorry", then it usually lacks authenticity.

Apologies often do not work because they do not achieve what the person expecting them wants to achieve:

> Manager: "What are you hoping that an apology will do for you?"
>
> Target: "I will feel better by hearing them admit that they were wrong. I will feel better knowing they had to apologise."

People who demand apologies from others often take a self-righteous position that is unhelpful in terms of restoration of relationship. Even when they get heartfelt apologies, they often cannot accept them because they doubt the sincerity of them. It is a minefield.

Then there are the obviously fake apologies:

- "I'm sorry for whatever I've done."
- "I'm sorry if you were offended."
- "I'm sorry if I did anything to hurt you."
- "I've said I'm sorry. Can we just move on?"

Fake apologies may be either too general or use the word "if" in a way that demonstrates a lack of ownership and accountability. In addition, the word "sorry" often minimises the damage done. This is one of the problems with apologies; even when they are given, they may not be received. They may leave the target with a sense of incomplete resolution.

What is important for healing and re-establishment of trust is not saying "sorry" as if it is a magic word. Showing genuine understanding and remorse by acknowledging what has occurred is more important:

> Manager: "What is important to you in seeking an apology. What do you really want?"
>
> Target: "I want them to understand how much they hurt me."
>
> Manager: "There might be a better process for that than an apology."

Recognition of hurt and the destructive impact of behaviour can come about by acknowledgement rather than apology. This is a different kind of gesture and usually more effective:

> Perpetrator: "I realise now after hearing you that what I did hurt you and created a barrier between us. I didn't realise this at the time because I was too wrapped up in my own drive to get certain results. I can see now that my actions created a lot of pain and humiliation for you. I feel remorseful for what I did, and I regret doing it now that I understand how it affected you."

There is no apology in this statement but instead an acknowledgement of responsibility and of the impact of behaviour and an expression of remorse. This is really what is important, not supporting a person to ride upon their high horse and demand the other grovel in humiliation by saying "sorry".

The goals of informal intervention processes are not punishment but restoration. Punishment appeals to another type of need. Restoration of relationship and re-establishment of trust are the focus of informal interventions.

Therefore, any informal intervention process should aim to allow people to be heard, understood, and acknowledged, and to ensure that genuine commitments are made about behaviour which are honoured into the future. If apologies are made, they need to be done well, otherwise the resolution process can be disrupted.

> In one situation two nurses had a three-year history of unresolved conflict. A previous mediation had failed to restore their relationship, and one nurse had filed a complaint against the other. The investigation failed to produce a finding, and the relationship became even worse to the point that neither could work together. A facilitator was brought in and worked with both nurses to create a working agreement. At the end of the process, the facilitator asked both nurses to attend a closure session, which would include their managers. The agreement would be read out and the facilitator would ask both nurses and their manager to make verbal commitments. The facilitator would then provide an opportunity for both nurses to say something to each other to bring about closure. They were asked to undertake a simple exercise: to acknowledge each other's pain. Each nurse was given some guidance,

and when the time came one nurse later confided that she was going to use the opportunity to vent her anger. The night before the session, the other nurse asked the facilitator if she could go first, and after discussing what she wanted to say the facilitator agreed. The next day, after reading out the agreements, the facilitator asked the first nurse to speak first. She pulled out a written statement and started by saying that, to her shame, she had not thought much about the other nurse's pain, because her own was so overwhelming. She went on to describe what she imagined the other nurse had experienced over the three years and how difficult this must have been. The other nurse, upon hearing an acknowledgement of her suffering, began to soften, and her eyes filled with tears. When it was her turn to speak, she had no anger left, and instead of attacking she expressed an acknowledgement of the first nurse's pain. Both nurses were able to come around from the protection of their defences and meet each other in a new way. It was the beginning of a new relationship.

¶10-040 Can leopards change their spots?

While leopards are genetically predisposed to have spots, bullies and harassers are not genetically predisposed to bully and harass. There is no evidence that people are born as bullies. Bullying and harassment are forms of behaviour that are learned, and they can be unlearned if a person is willing. People can change if they want to change, and this can be supported by an organisation that takes this seriously. If a person will not change, then they will continue to use bullying and harassment. An organisation must decide how much damage they are prepared to accept.

The issue of change needs to be understood by organisations. According to proponents of motivational interviewing, change is a process that has specific stages, and people can become stuck at one of those stages, thus not achieving completeness until they have gone through all the stages, one by one. Change takes time and it requires ongoing motivation and support.

What motivates bullies to change? It is not usually the fear of punishment. If the fear of punishment stopped people committing crimes, then our jails would be empty. The fear of punishment is not a great demotivator for crime, nor is it for bullying.

What does prevent bullying and harassment is empathy. When someone understands at a felt level the impact their behaviour has had on another person, it is the most powerful demotivator for bullying and harassment. This is the main reason why most people don't bully or harass others. They don't want to hurt someone or make them afraid. They don't want to cause suffering. Therefore, informal interventions can have long-lasting effects, because they allow for empathy to be cultivated.

Another effective demotivator for bullying and harassment is image. People generally want to look good and do not want to be thought of as bullies or harassers. These are not characteristics that people want attributed to them, therefore a person can be motivated to change their behaviour accordingly, so they maintain a good image.

Another effective demotivator for bullying and harassment is alignment to values and beliefs. When people adopt clear values about safety, dignity, and respect in their lives, this can demotivate them from bullying or harassing. However, some people still bully and harass even when they have espoused values to the contrary.

However, the best demotivator is empathy: the ability to connect with and identify with another person's experience, to be able to put oneself in another person's shoes. As Mary T. Lathrap's poem "Judge Softly" says:

> "Pray, don't find fault with the man that limps
>
> Or stumbles along the road.
>
> Unless you have worn the moccasins he wears
>
> Or stumbled beneath the same load."

Therefore, the 4 levels of demotivation are:

1. I might get into trouble. (punishment)
2. I will not look good as a person. It won't be good for my reputation. (social)
3. It is against my values and beliefs. (values)
4. I don't want to hurt them. I wouldn't want to experience that myself. (empathy)

The most powerful demotivator is empathy.

¶10-050 Developing empathy

The ability to empathise is often espoused as a quality of emotional intelligence. When a person lacks empathy, they struggle to understand how people feel and how people are. They objectify people and shut themselves off from them. They do things without considering how they will damage others, because they are insulated. There is a disconnection at a feeling and experience level. People who lack empathy often do things or say things that hurt, frighten or offend others and have no understanding of how they affect others. People who lack empathy may also find it difficult to experience their own emotions and make sense of them. If a person cannot relate to their own internal experience and understand why they feel the way they do, it is understandable that they will fail to relate to the experience of others.

Practising role reversal can assist people to develop empathy. This is a technique from the fields of psychodrama and sociodrama and is widely used in various psychotherapeutic fields of study.

Role reversal is an exercise that involves putting yourself in another person's position and relating to events as if you are the other person:

> "Before you dish that behaviour out to me, come and feel what it's like on the receiving end."

Role reversal enables people to experience what it's like to be on the receiving end of words, actions and expressions. One version of this is the empty chair process, where a person sits opposite an empty chair. They speak to the empty chair and express themselves. Then they change chairs. The facilitator takes up the role and expresses the person's initial expression. The person who has moved to the empty chair is now on the receiving end. They get a sense of what it's like to be the recipient. This pattern may continue with different attempts at expression so the person can gain a new sense of how they "come across". It is a simple tool to help develop empathy.

Within organisations there are huge opportunities for people to develop empathy. It starts with being able to talk about emotions and thoughts, to develop the language that accurately describes what is going on under the surface. It begins by learning to listen and identify with others as people.

Organisations are not machines, and the people in them are not cogs. We are all living, feeling, creative beings who are authentically able to connect with each other. You cannot leave your emotions at the door when you go to work, but if you can incorporate them, explore them, and use them to enhance the sense of collective functioning, then this enhances relationships and increases the possibility of cooperation and synergy.

Providing opportunity to develop the capacity for empathy is crucial if organisations want to be free of bullying and harassment. One person in a training course made a case for the development of empathy by saying:

> "No-one really cares what I feel or think here. There is no time for reflection or talking at anything more than a superficial level. People here relate to each other as tools that do jobs. I hate it, but I do it too. Productivity and sorting out problems are the main topics of conversation. I no longer feel that I can endure this kind of environment. It's not that I feel bullied, although some are, but the whole culture is dehumanising. It's like no-one feels anything and no-one relates on that level."

Empathy can be learned. People can develop the awareness critical to its development. Managers and supervisors can take some time to listen to people and to reflect on experiences that people have. They can enquire and respond empathetically.

Some people who struggle to empathise can learn mechanical empathy. This is a skill of recognising how someone might be feeling by relating to non-verbal cues such as facial expressions, body language, words and tones of voice.

Empathy is crucial if organisations want to prevent bullying and harassment.

Chapter 11

How to Conduct Informal Interventions

¶11-010 The 4 types of informal interventions

This chapter addresses the way to conduct 4 specific types of informal interventions:

- manager-directed resolution
- facilitated conversations
- round-table facilitation
- team functioning reviews.

Each of these processes is different and can be effective in assisting people to resolve bullying and harassment concerns.

¶11-020 Informal intervention 1: Manager-directed resolution

One of the simplest types of informal intervention is the manager-directed resolution.

The manager listens to both parties separately, comes to some accurate conclusions about the issues and behaviours of concern, and then sets some clear expectations for the parties to abide by. The manager listens first, then tells people what to do and what not to do.

Although this intervention might appear quite authoritarian, it can achieve behavioural results. The manager acts as a fair-minded judge who directs the resolution and sets expectations for future interaction.

The process involves some specific steps:

1. The concerned person approaches the manager, and the manager gains an understanding of this person's concerns. The behaviours of concern are identified by going through the EXPLORE model, the effects, needs, and preferred behaviours are also identified. A plan is devised, and an agreement is made for the manager to progress by talking separately with the other person.
2. The manager meets with the person of concern (the other person) and enquires about their relationship with the concerned person. The manager can explain that the concerned person has raised concerns. It is important that the manager is factual when relaying the other person's

concerns and does not embellish or colour the facts with their own interpretation.

3. The manager hears the responses of the person of concern.
4. The manager reflects on each person's needs and concerns as well as any other issues that require attention. The manager creates a list of behavioural expectations. This can be put in writing but does not make specific allegations against anyone in particular.
5. The manager meets again with the concerned person and explains the responses. The manager explains the set of expectations and conveys this to the concerned person.
6. The manager also provides this to the person of concern.
7. The manager requests a meeting of the parties to finalise the matter. The expectations are explained, and the parties are given a chance to express commitments. Or the manager requests the parties meet together themselves privately and express commitments The manager checks to see if this occurs.
8. The manager keeps personal notes of what has been agreed to and uses this as a basis to follow up and ensure the agreements have been adhered to.

¶11-030 Case study example

An employee approached her manager about her new team leader. The employee discussed a few incidents that had occurred between herself and the team leader that had disturbed her. The manager listened and clarified the types of behaviour that had allegedly occurred and the impact on the employee, and then agreed on a plan to resolve matters. The plan was:

- The manger would talk to the team leader and explain that the employee had raised concerns. The manager would describe the types of behaviour the employee had raised concerns about and how they affected the employee.
- The manager would then hear the team leader's perspective.
- The manager would then provide feedback to the employee about the team leader's responses and discuss the next steps.

The concerned person wanted some personal support, and the manager arranged a counsellor.

Next, the manager asked the team leader to her office. She discussed with the team leader the concerns that had been raised by the employee and enquired into the manager's motivation and behaviour. When she noticed that the team leader was open and willing to address the situation, the manager suggested a plan. The team leader would approach the employee on her own and address the concerns in private. She would be acknowledging the specific behavioural concerns and make a commitment about alternative ways of communicating in the future. The goal would be an agreement about the future and an acknowledgement of the effects of the past behaviour. The manager coached the team leader on how to conduct the meeting with the employee.

The manager then phoned the concerned employee and discussed the suggested plan. The employee expressed concern at having a direct conversation with the team leader, and the manager told her that if at any time things became uncomfortable she should stop the meeting and phone the manager, who would intervene directly.

The employee wanted to bring a support person to the meeting, but the manager was concerned that this would produce an imbalance. This would be a feature expected in a formal process; however, this was an informal meeting. The manager also reiterated that after the meeting with the team leader the manager would follow up on what had happened with both parties. These commitments gave some comfort to the employee.

The meeting took place, and the team leader addressed the employee's concerns and sought to resolve matters. The employee appreciated the meeting and the team leader's acknowledgements. Agreements were made between them regarding how they would work together in the future.

The manager met with the team leader and the employee after their meeting and enquired about how the meeting had transpired. Both parties said the meeting went well. It was agreed that the manager would check in after a month to see how both parties were and gave assurances that if anything further arose either party could approach her.

The intervention was successful because:

- The manager listened to both parties and formulated an accurate understanding of the issues, and behaviours concerned.
- The manager directed a resolution process and coached both parties on how to conduct themselves.
- The manager did not complicate matters by allowing support persons present or putting the employee's concerns in writing.
- The manager made specific commitments regarding personal support and intervention.
- The manager followed up and ensured that matters were resolved.

An important principle is involved in informal interventions. Keep matters simple and resolve issues at the lowest level possible. Provide support but don't treat people as helpless or unable to speak for themselves.

Support people can derail a meeting if they act in an adversarial way. The manager did not know how the support person might respond in the meeting. If she had agreed to allowing one party to bring a support person, the manager would also need to have notified the team leader of this. The team leader might also have asked for a support person, since it would otherwise have become one-sided. This could have unnecessarily complicated matters and raised tension.

Is it risky to allow private meetings to happen after someone has been bullied?

It can be, but it can also work well if the team leader and the employee behave constructively. The manager needed to make a judgment about that. It is important to restate that this kind of intervention is not always appropriate. The manager chose to conduct this process because she had confidence in the team leader and the employee. In other situations, she might be more directly involved.

¶11-040 Informal intervention 2: Facilitated conversations

The process of facilitating a conversation between 2 people involves some clear process steps and safeguards. These can be learned by any manager. Even children in schools conduct facilitated discussions between their peers. This process is often called peer mediation.

Facilitated discussions are processes that allow people to speak with each other and resolve their concerns in the presence of a third party who controls the process.

There is always some risk in facilitated discussions because sometimes there are strong emotions and unless people have been coached and are prepared things can go awry.

The manager's job is to prepare the people for the discussion, assess their readiness to engage, coach where needed, and then conduct the process in a safe and productive way.

There are 2 main forms that facilitated discussions can take as processes used to resolve concerns about bullying or harassment.

The first form of this is very structured to maintain control and avoid harmful outbursts or other destructive behaviour. This is important, otherwise the process may deteriorate into a fight or a walk-out by someone. The manager should not allow this to occur.

Instead of expressing anger, people are encouraged to describe their anger. This is to give the other person the opportunity to empathise and understand them.

Both forms of facilitated discussions described in this chapter begin with independent meetings with the people concerned. The EXPLORE model is used to prepare people and to help the facilitator establish understanding and trust.

¶11-050 Case study example

A first-line supervisor had a longstanding grievance against his senior manager, 2 levels up. The supervisor spoke to a facilitator about his opinion of the senior manager. When the facilitator commented on the anger and resentment expressed, the supervisor explained the history of their relationship. Seven years earlier, the supervisor had been subjected to a complaint and a disciplinary process for misconduct. The process had been conducted by the senior manager, and some tense exchanges between them at the time had been experienced by the supervisor as unnecessarily hurtful and demeaning. After the disciplinary process was completed, the supervisor held resentment against the manager. This had continued till the present day.

The facilitator used the EXPLORE model to understand the actual behaviours, the impact, and the preferred behaviour. When he asked the supervisor what he would like to see happen, the supervisor became thoughtful and said he was tired of carrying the resentment and wished he could have a better kind of relationship with the manager. The facilitator spoke about the options, including self-help or an informal intervention such as a facilitated discussion.

The supervisor became interested in the possibility of a facilitated discussion. The facilitator described the process that would take place. The supervisor would have the opportunity to speak about the past and how it affected him. The facilitator would request that the manager listen without responding or interrupting. There would be a pause in the meeting, and both parties would separate so the facilitator could check to see what the manager's response was. Then, if ready, they would return to the meeting, and the facilitator would allow the manager to speak and respond. After this was completed, the process would then involve discussion about the future and possible commitments that could be made between them.

The process was agreed, and the facilitator described what would be necessary to progress:

- Both parties need to agree on the process.
- The purpose was to improve their working relationship by clearing up past issues and making genuine commitments for the benefit of them both and of the organisation.
- The facilitator would oversee the process and would interrupt proceedings, if necessary, to ensure the conversations were constructive.
- Both parties would speak with the aim of being understood, not to vent anger or abuse or to harm the other person.
- Both parties would listen with the goal of understanding the other person. This meant allowing the other person to be honest and describe their feelings and thoughts.
- Both parties would take responsibility for their own feelings, thoughts and actions and refrain from blaming the other person for them.

The facilitator asked the supervisor to prepare himself, and the supervisor asked if he could write his thoughts on paper and discuss this with the facilitator prior to the meeting. This was agreed.

The facilitator then approached the senior manager. He asked how she felt about the relationship between her and the supervisor. The manager expressed frustration and disappointment that the relationship was fraught and had been this way for years. The facilitator explained that he had discussed this with the supervisor, and he had become interested in a way to talk and resolve things. The manager expressed some interest but wanted to know more. The facilitator explained that matters began from an incident 7 years before.

The facilitator asked the manager to describe what had happened. He heard the senior manager's account. The facilitator shared enough, without disclosing the supervisor's complete experience, to ensure the manager would be curious to know more.

The manager grew more interested in resolving the longstanding dispute between them. This led to an agreement to continue with the facilitated discussion, and the same list of requirements were discussed and agreed to. Times and dates were discussed. The facilitator would meet with both parties individually prior to the meeting.

The supervisor prepared himself for the session by writing out what he wanted to say. He read this to the facilitator prior to the meeting. The facilitator gave feedback and assisted the supervisor to express himself openly and honestly. This strengthened the supervisor's confidence. It also assured the facilitator that he would be able to describe his feelings rather than express them in an unproductive way.

The facilitator met with both parties shortly before the meeting. He checked that both understood how the process would happen and that they would allow the facilitator to direct the discussion.

The supervisor started the process. He described that he had held resentment over many years and that he didn't want to do that anymore. Then he described the source of his resentment, said that he had been hurt by comments, and described the manager's behaviour that he had interpreted as dismissive and demeaning. He described how he had hardened his attitude toward the manager and behaved with anger. He admitted he had been quite abusive at times. He said he had put up a wall between them and had been critical of the manager. He also explained that he had hoped the manager might reach out to him to talk about it, but never did.

The manager sat listening without interrupting, fidgeting, or responding physically. Suitable eye contact was maintained. The supervisor finished by saying he hoped that this could be resolved.

The facilitator stopped the meeting and asked the supervisor to leave the room temporarily.

The facilitator then asked the manager to describe her experience of sitting and listening. The manager breathed a sigh of relief and said she was grateful for this opportunity. They talked about her experience, and the facilitator coached her on how to respond when the supervisor returned. The facilitator was confident the manager could respond with empathy.

When the supervisor was asked to return to the meeting, the facilitator asked the manager to speak and asked the supervisor to listen. The manager did so with empathy and by also being open about her experience of the past. She thanked the supervisor for bravely expressing himself and she acknowledged that she had not reached out because she had lacked confidence about what to do. She added that she wished she had done so now.

The facilitator noted that both parties were open with each other and had expressed themselves about what mattered to them. There was a free expression of emotions and respect for each other. He then asked them both to describe how they wanted their relationship to be from here on. This involved some specific agreements that each said they would commit themselves to, involving communication and mutual support.

The session took 2 hours. Preparation involved 3 hours of the facilitator's time.

¶11-060 Significant aspects

It is important for the facilitator to help prepare people to communicate. Never assume that people will know how to express themselves constructively. They may need time to work through emotions and get themselves into a constructive place, where they can explain themselves rather than get caught up in attacking or defending.

The facilitator must control the process strictly to ensure that it does not deteriorate. The start is very important. Both people need to know what to do and what to expect in a general way. The facilitator needs to be ready to interrupt any behaviour that is unhelpful.

What if the manager had not been able to relate to the supervisor's initial statements?

If this had been the case, the facilitator would have needed to coach the supervisor until he was able to listen without reacting. If the facilitator had not been confident about this, it might have been necessary to stop proceedings at this point and explain that there would be a postponement until the manager was ready to continue.

What if the manager had disagreed with the events as the supervisor had recalled them?

It is important that people do not get into an argument about the facts of past events. If they disagree significantly on events, then this can be acknowledged and clarified. However, the exercise is not to test the accuracy of people's memories but to understand events as they experienced them and the impact they had.

Studies show that people often remember only facets of events, and the memories becomes embedded and remembered as facts. It is important for people to be able to talk about their memory of past events without demanding that they are right and other person is wrong. Sometimes people end up agreeing to disagree, but they can still understand how someone has been affected.

Why was it important for the manager not to respond during the first phase of the meeting when the supervisor was describing what had happened and how she had been affected?

Sometimes people respond and interrupt the person who is speaking. Their reactions can send messages that the first person might not accurately interpret. A headshake, a rolling of the eyes, a look of disbelief, a snorting or a sniffing can all be interpreted negatively. It is better to leave the responses to the next stage of the meeting. Delaying responses means the person who listens focuses on listening and understanding the experience of the other person.

A reasonable level of eye contact is important. It depends on the amount of eye contact being displayed by the first person speaking. It is not necessary for people to stare into each other's eyes all the time, but no eye contact can be interpreted as not listening.

This kind of facilitated discussion has distinct phases and allows the facilitator to coach each person. It prevents escalation, and it creates space and time for dialogue and understanding. It is usually a powerful and empowering experience for people.

The second type of facilitated discussion is less structured. It is appropriate when the level of emotion is not as high. It avoids having a break in proceedings after the first person has spoken.

This type of facilitated discussion involves 3 stages:

The preparation stage is where the parties work at how they will present themselves and what the role of the facilitator will be. The manager listens to both parties separately and makes an assessment about the concerns and issues raised. If the manager considers the parties are ready to meet in a direct way, the manager brings them together and facilitates a process of communication.

The second stage is where both parties get a chance to speak about their concerns, including what has happened and how they have been affected. Each party listens and then responds when directed by the facilitator.

1. The facilitator opens the meeting and thanks both parties for agreeing to talk.
2. The facilitator describes the purpose of the meeting. This should be worded in a way that clarifies the work to be done.
3. The facilitator clarifies the rules of engagement. Typical rules might include:
    - No violence, abuse or attacking.
    - Let people have their say without interrupting.
    - Listen and try to understand each other's experience and perspectives.
    - If you need a break, ask for it.
    - Take responsibility for your own behaviour.
4. The facilitator invites the first person to speak about what has happened, and how they have been affected.

The facilitator should be ready to intervene if matters become disruptive. If the first person begins to verbally attack the other person or makes specific judgments about the other person that are based on negative assumptions, the facilitator should step in and ask this person to restate their position without making assumptions about the other person.

Once finished, the facilitator can briefly summarise the content and specific points the first person has made. This reinforces that the issues have been described and laid out accurately.

5. The facilitator then invites the second person to respond, first by acknowledging the concerns expressed by the first person, and secondly by explaining any issues they have. The first person now listens.
6. At the end of the second person's statement, the facilitator summarises what has been said and acknowledged.
7. The facilitator asks the first person to acknowledge what has been said by the second person.

In this phase of the facilitated discussion, it is important for each person to be heard and acknowledged. Taking responsibility for behaviour and actions, even if there may be some differences in memory, is important. It is important also to clarify intentions in the past and the present.

The third phase involves discussion about what is needed to resolve matters. The facilitator might start by asking each person to describe what is important to them in order to move on, and what needs to happen to sort the issues out and reach a place of mutual respect and cooperation. The discussion shifts from describing concerns and impacts to describing what is the most important needs for each person. This is a negotiation stage, and it ends when commitments and agreements have been reached.

Agreements are important. They are a foundation for trust to be re-established. They may include specific things that people will do as well as more general aspects. An example of an agreement might be:

Agreement between Person 1 and Person 2.

- We will show respect toward each other.
- We will cooperate with each other.
- We will refrain from the following types of behaviour:
  - displays of aggression
  - bad-mouthing.
- If an issue arises, we will discuss and, if necessary, will continue a facilitated discussion.

Signed by parties and facilitator:

Date:

Agreements can be kept on file. They solidify the commitments that have been made. They are also useful when a manager checks up to see how the parties are maintaining their commitments.

Agreements should never apportion blame. Instead, they should focus on what the parties want and expect from each other. They cannot be used later in a formal proceeding as evidence that one person used bullying behaviour.

The process begins with one party describing their issues. It ends with a working agreement, acknowledgements, and a support and monitoring process. If the agreement fails, it can be revisited, or a person can choose to take the matter to a formal complaint.

¶11-070 Informal intervention 3: Round-table facilitation

This process is useful when there are more than 2 people involved in the situation or when the people involved request that others are present.

For example, there might be the 2 main parties who want to find resolution, as well as their manager, an HR manager, and the union delegate. It is important that each person has a reason for being there and understands their role in the proceedings.

The facilitator should meet with each person prior to the meeting and brief them on their role and the purpose of the meeting. This helps the facilitator understand the issues as each person sees them and it also assists in creating trust between the facilitator and each person.

When the meeting begins, the facilitator should describe the purpose clearly.

> "We are meeting here to resolve something that seems to have been going on for some time and has had an impact on several different people. You are here because the main parties think it's important to involve you. Some past events need to be talked about to reach an understanding of how people have been affected by them. As a group, you need to think about how this matter can be dealt with so that everyone can move on with the hope of resolution. Are you willing to take part in this?"

The facilitator needs to confirm that everyone is committed to the purpose. If one person has a different reason for being in the meeting, that person may shut themselves out or hijack the meeting.

For example, if one person is resentful and wants to demand a different process or outcome, then it is best if this is declared at the beginning. The facilitator can then choose to ask them to leave or ask them to put aside their agenda.

Next, the facilitator needs to explain some rules of engagement so that everyone is clear about how to behave themselves. The term "rules of engagement" can be described as guidelines for interaction or some other terminology.

The key point is that the facilitator clarifies 2 main things: the purpose (what we are here to do) and the culture (how we will engage to best achieve the purpose).

The first phase is where people get to express what they see as the main issues and how these issues have affected them personally.

Each person explains their perspective, and after each person has spoken the facilitator summarises the main issues and the effects. A whiteboard can be a useful tool so that everything is visible to everyone.

The second phase involves focusing on the needs level:

> "We have explored what has happened and how that has been viewed by each of you. We have explored how past events have affected people. Now let's focus on what you think are the main needs that require attention. I would like to hear your views on this."

The facilitator might choose people and ask them to speak or get people to speak in turn. Everyone should be able to speak and offer their view. This will naturally create some ideas about what to do next.

The third phase is a chance for people to discuss possible solutions and how the needs can be met. This is the creative phase where people offer ideas and brainstorm solutions.

The last phase is where people determine what will happen from this point onwards. They create a plan to guide the future. Agreements about this are recorded.

When a group has endured a manager who has bullied them, and now this manager has left, this process can be a useful opportunity for people to express themselves about the past and talk about how they want things to change:

> "Thank you for coming. This meeting is an opportunity to talk about the past, the present, and the future. Let's start with the past and talk about how you have been affected by what has happened. When we have done that, let's see how everyone is in the present and explore that. Then we will look to the future and talk about what you need as a team."

In one team people found it very difficult to start to talk about what had happened. The group seemed frozen until one person began to weep. Others offered comfort, and this created an opportunity for people to speak about their experiences. The facilitator was reluctant to hurry on too quickly, realising there was much more in the group that needed to be expressed. After 2 hours, people had cried, vented anger, expressed grief and sadness, talked about their guilt for not doing enough, and emptied a box of tissues. Everyone had spoken, and the ice had melted. The facilitator called a break and asked that people stay silent and not talk further with each other but wait until the group returned. When they came back from the break, the facilitator asked them to talk about what they were experiencing in themselves in the present moment. People talked about feeling relieved and lighter. Some people felt a sense of compassion for others. Some people laughed. This took about half an hour, and the facilitator then asked people to think about the future they wanted and needed from this point. Everyone agreed that they did not want another bullying experience but instead a future where they felt supported and respected. They wanted to be a team again. The group developed a charter for the year ahead and made specific commitments to action items.

¶11-080 Informal intervention 4: Team functioning review

This informal intervention is especially useful when there is reasonable cause to believe that bullying or harassment is occurring within a work team, but the people are not willing to make a complaint.

The main reason why people do not wish to follow through to a resolution process is that they are distrusting and afraid. They may be afraid of what will happen and how safe they will be. While they may be courageous enough to talk about what is happening to an external person, they do not want to be the one who initiates a complaint.

This is evidence of a significant shadow within a work team. There will be a climate of fear, a code of silence and polarisation. People may have adopted roles that support the perpetrators or support the targets. There will be some people who want to avoid getting involved and stay neutral. Their personal reluctance to speak up might have been beneficial for them amid the circumstances they faced.

> In one team, two people spoke to an independent trainer about the bullying that was occurring. The trainer encouraged them to speak with the general manager. They did this, and the general manager asked them to make complaints so he could conduct an investigation. They both said they would not make a complaint because they feared the backlash for doing so. Instead, they both spoke of resigning from the workplace. The general manager spoke to an external facilitator for advice, and the facilitator suggested an informal review of the team as a way of understanding the dynamics and bringing people to a place of action.

The normal process of a team review is to interview everyone individually, asking each person the same questions, then summarising the answers and mixing them up to protect the identities of the people involved. The final document is then published and given to team members so that everyone can see what everyone else has submitted. After this, a team meeting can be held to discuss what people in the team want and to solidify that into a charter for the team.

Typical questions in a team review might include:

- What words would you use to describe how this team functions?
- Name 3 things people do in this team that you like or appreciate.
- What 3 things do people do in this team that you don't like or appreciate?
- How would you rate this team from 1 (low) – 10 (high) on the following criteria?
    - productivity and efficiency
    - cohesion
    - trust
    - supportiveness
    - safety
    - communication
    - leadership.

It is important that there is no specific review of the manager or team leader of the group, unless that has been specifically requested. However, there is a question on leadership. Leadership is often something expected of management, but anyone in a group can show leadership. Leadership is a function, not a position. In a healthy team, leadership shows up regularly, but in a toxic team leadership is absent.

The information gathered from the interviews provides a view of overall team functioning from everyone's perspectives. Everyone gets to see what the summary of answers is. No one is identified. Confidentiality is maintained for the sake of safety.

The day after people have viewed the material, the facilitator can gather the group together to discuss the team review and their responses to it. In this meeting the facilitator needs to ensure the group develops a clear purpose and explain that there are some guidelines for discussion to ensure people are safe.

> The general manager agreed to the team review process and sent a memo to the team and team leader announcing that the facilitator would be arriving to conduct individual interviews. The night before, one team member confronted the general manager and angrily demanded to know why this was happening. The general manager explained there had been high staff turnover in the team during the last few years and that concerns had been raised about the team dynamics. The team member became angrier and threatened to resign if the facilitator was brought in. The general manager would not back down, and in the heat of the moment the team member resigned on the spot. The next day, the facilitator met with the other team members. During the interviews, the two people who had initially raised concerns decided to make formal complaints. They explained that the person who resigned was the worst bully in the team and that now she had left they were more confident to speak up about another person in the team who allegedly supported the main perpetrator. The team review process was postponed and an investigation process started. During the investigation, the other respondent resigned. This meant that both people accused of bullying had resigned from the team. The team leader also confessed to allowing the bullying to occur because he had been threatened by the two people accused of bullying.

Team reviews provide an opportunity for people to begin to talk about the health of the team, and it allows people to safely describe what is happening. The goal of a team review is to improve team functioning. The focus is on behaviour rather than personalities. Team reviews can allow things that might normally not be expressed to be raised.

Chapter 12

Troubleshooting

¶12-010 A framework for analysis

This chapter discusses ways to approach situations involving bullying and harassment. Managers or facilitators may be asked to make assessments and intervene in group situations where matters have become difficult.

It is important for a manager or facilitator to make an analysis of what is happening in the group and understand the forces that are at work. This requires thinking about a group or team as a system. A team functions as a system of interconnected parts, like a living machine.

Unless a manager can make an accurate assessment of what is happening in the system, it will be difficult to create significant change. Instead, a manager's actions may even reinforce the dynamics and make them worse.

A basic framework for analysis is:

1. Listen to a wide range of people in the group before developing any hypotheses. The direct manager's view of the problem is one view, but it will not be everyone's view of the "how things are". Try to talk to everyone, and if that is not possible speak to representatives of each group so that you get a view based on a range of perceptions.
2. Clarify the structure of the group and the hierarchy. Who manages who? Who has responsibility? How are decisions made? Who has agency and power? Is the management style authoritarian or laissez-faire? What's the balance between autocracy and democracy?
3. Find out who is doing what. Who are players that are enacting bullying roles? Who are the targets? Who supports the targets? Who supports the perpetrators? Who tries to stay neutral by avoiding taking sides? What roles do people enact? What sort of bullying or harassing behaviours are occurring?
4. How do people relate together in this group? Who are the influencers or leaders? Who is popular? Who is unpopular? Who are the isolated individuals who are disconnected?
5. Is it an open or a closed system? In a closed system people become stuck and rigid. There is nothing fresh coming in. They may be despairing and negative. Open systems are more open and flexible. How open are people to learn, to receive feedback, and to change?

6. What are the issues of the group? What are they angry and upset about? What are they afraid of? What do they hope for? What needs are not being met?
7. What are the beliefs of the group or the unwritten rules of the group? What are the common values of the group?
8. What is the history of the group? What are the group stories and narratives?
9. What is missing in the group? What is not happening or not allowed to happen?

This is a way of examining a group as a system of forces. It can inform a facilitator of the best way to approach things.

Sometimes a training session can be a useful way to start. In other situations, individual interviews are more useful. Sometimes groups interviews are best. Sometimes a confidential survey is necessary. Sometimes a facilitator might work with a sub-group or the first-line manager. Each group is different and may respond to matters differently.

> In one organisation a facilitator was asked to provide a training session on bullying and harassment. When he arrived, the manager explained nervously that group members were upset. Rather than try to suppress the emotions, the facilitator wanted to provide room for them to be expressed. The facilitator asked for the chairs to be arranged in the training room in a circle, so that everyone could see each other's faces.
>
> The facilitator noticed people's body language as they entered the room. This indicated that people were tense and possibly angry. The manger introduced the facilitator. Immediately, two people in the group asked why they had been told to attend the session. Another asked what the point was. It was a dramatic start.
>
> The manager looked nervous and asked the facilitator to start, then sat down. In a game of rugby this is often called a "hospital pass". The person catching the pass is immediately flattened by a tackler. Everything depended on what the facilitator did next. The facilitator stood up and spoke slowly as he looked around the room of angry faces:
>
>> "It sounds like some of you are quite grumpy here today. I am interested in understanding why that is. Before we discuss anything about bullying and harassment, I want to give each of you an opportunity to talk about what is on your mind as you sit here right now."
>
> People began to speak one by one around the room, and the facilitator responded empathetically, noting specific issues on a whiteboard. By the time everyone had spoken, the mood had lifted. Listening had created a shift.

People usually want to be heard. They want to speak about what is bothering them. A reflective listener will focus on words, music and dance:

- Words are the language people use.
- Music is the sound of the speaking, including tone, pace, emphasis and volume.
- Dance is the expression of the body, including facial expressions, hand and body movement, eyes, and even breathing.

These are modes of communication and they each express what is being experienced by a person. Words are the least reliable, because people can easily lie with words, but the music and dance are often more reliable. A good listener hears what is being said but also how it is being said. A good listener is not just listening but seeing and feeling as well. When a listener reflects what is being communicated, the person communicating will feel seen and heard. The communicator may not even be aware of the depth of their own experience until a listener reflects it back to them.

A good listener will be able to understand a person's thoughts and feelings, but also their intentions, motivations, values and beliefs. They will read the whole person, not just one part. Doing this allows the person communicating to become more deeply aware of themselves. This is how people can connect with each other. When one person communicates openly and is seen and heard, it will inspire others to do the same.

When people are angry about something, a good listener will detect more than the anger, but also the other primary emotions under the anger. If the listener acknowledges these other emotions, the anger will dissipate, and the person will become aware of themselves in a deeper way. This increases their self-awareness and allows them to present themselves in a clear way. The mood can change quickly, and the focus can move to areas that are crucial to resolve matters.

> Person: "Management is the problem here. It's all about control and manipulation. They don't want to talk, and they sure don't listen. That's where the bullying is coming from. I have had enough, and to be told to come here and learn about bullying is a joke!"
>
> Facilitator: "You began by expressing some anger about management, but as you speak I see that you are concerned about the team as a whole, and there are one or two people you have been flicking your eyes toward as you have been speaking. I initially thought you might be seeking their approval, but now I think you are ensuring they are included. You care about them, and maybe you want to hear from them?"
>
> Person: "I am one of the senior people here. I have seen this before. But, yes, I am concerned about the younger ones and the effect of this on

them and their families. They are being used as pawns. This is breaking us as a team, and we need to work together rather than as individuals."

Facilitator: "So speak to them directly and let them know what you care about and what you want."

Person: (to others in the team) "I want to hear what you think. Where are you at in this?"

The work of facilitation is about providing opportunities for people to speak honestly to each other and hear each other. Direct communication encourages more direct communication. Things that have been held back become exposed, and real issues are brought into the open. Silent elephants in the room shrink in size when they are brought into the open. This changes the dynamics. When people speak and listen, they often find common ground and can then make commitments and agreements that are important for healthy team dynamics.

¶12-020 Healthy team model

A useful model for assessing the health of a team involves 3 main elements: trust, cohesion, and mutuality.

These 3 elements exist in a connected way and when these elements are strong, it indicates a healthy team dynamic. When they are weak, it indicates an unhealthy team dynamic. Teams either function or they dysfunction. These things are in a balance. When teams function, people achieve things in a synergistic way. Synergy is a term that describes the dynamics of people working powerfully as one. When a team is dysfunctional, the people in the teams focus on coping mechanisms. This decreases creativity and innovation.

Teams are constantly moving with change, tensions, conflicts and challenges. Some teams become dysfunctional and stay that way for a long time. Some get stuck in an adversarial, combative, defensive way of being. Bullying becomes more predominant in these teams.

This is not inevitable, and things can be done to improve the situation. Sociometry is a qualitative method for measuring social relationships. It was developed by Jacob L. Moreno and Helen Hall Jennings in their studies of the relationship between social structures and psychological well-being and is used during "remedial teaching". The better the sociometry, the better the group maintains itself and bounces back from difficult experiences.

If managers understand some basic features of group sociometry and what it takes to improve things, this can lead to improved communication, cooperation and productivity.

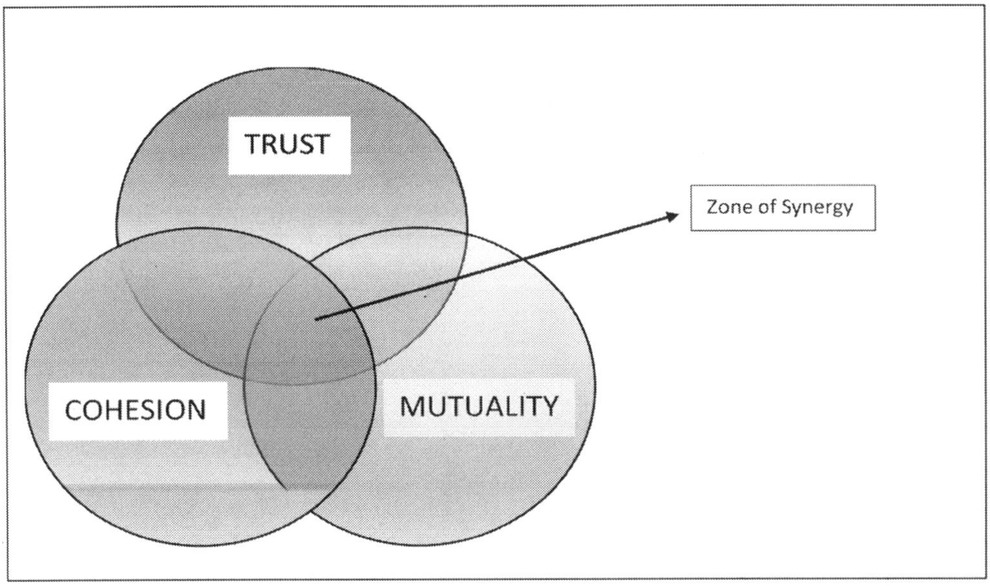

¶12-030 Trust

Trust is an interesting phenomenon. It is something that people feel, and it is also something that people do. If someone feels trusted, they may offer trust. When they feel trust, they give trust in return and become more trustworthy:

> "I trust you to do this. I have confidence that you will not let me down."

The opposite is also true. When people feel distrust, they offer distrust in return. Trust is like a commodity or a currency. It gets passed back and forward. Distrust is like bad debt.

When people trust each other, their sociometry improves. Trust is faith or confidence in something of value. Distrust is confidence in something disappointing.

There are 2 main types of ground that trust grows in. Firstly, trust grows in the ground of openness and honesty. When people are open and honest with each other, trust usually starts to grow. Even if the news is bad, it is still the truth and useful. If you explain to me how you feel about something and what your thoughts and intentions are, I know where you are at and what you are up to. I get a clear picture of you. I will develop trust in you because you are being honest with me.

Most people want to know where they are at in relation to others. When someone gives feedback, the other person knows how they are viewed by the other person. If a person doesn't get feedback, they don't know what the person thinks of them. They will develop distrust.

In any war, the first casualty is the truth. People stop telling the truth and present false information, propaganda, and gas-lighting instead. This creates distrust.

In conflict people stop talking openly. They want to avoid unpleasantness. Instead of describing and talking about how they feel, they often express their feelings as a weapon against the other person. They make judgments, accuse, insult or blame. Sometimes they clam up and communicate with passive-aggression such as sulking, moodiness, sarcasm, negativity and dismissive contempt. This creates distrust. Lying is the worst enemy of trust:

> "Because you have lied to me, I cannot trust you anymore."

> "If you never give me feedback about the work I do, I won't know where I stand with you and I will end up wondering if you trust me and if I can trust you."

If you want to improve trust in a relationship, start talking honestly about yourself and what you are doing or wanting. Start opening up and revealing yourself. Not in an insulting way, but in a clear way so other people know where you are at. Also, start asking open questions of the other person:

> "How do you feel about this?"

> "What is important to you?"

Sometimes people don't know how to be open and honest without being insulting or judgmental. It may take some work to figure out how to be open and honest without dumping on someone, but it is important. It is also important that people listen without taking offence and making negative assumptions:

> "Speak to create understanding and listen to understand."

The second ground that trust grows in is the ground of commitment. People develop trust when they make and honour commitments. If I agree to do something and then follow through by doing it, you will trust me. I am upholding my word. If I make a commitment to do something but don't follow through, then you will distrust me. In mediation, it is important to get people being honest with each other and then making and honouring commitments toward each other. It is important to create trust.

Making a commitment is like planting a seed; honouring that commitment is the seed growing to be seen. Actions speak louder than words.

In a high-trust relationship people trust each other and they make commitments to each other. If someone says they will be arriving at 3pm, and then realise they cannot make it until 4pm, then it is up to them to communicate and make a new commitment. If they just turn up an hour late, it will create distrust. Those who make commitments should take responsibility to maintain the commitment and revisit it if necessary.

¶12-040 Cohesion

Cohesion is a factor of flow in relationships. It is the ability to flow with each other and stay in relationship with each other despite the ups and downs of life. When people are cohesive, they flow without friction. They don't "rub each up the wrong way" or do things that create friction with the other person.

To develop cohesiveness in a relationship, people need to get to know each other and learn about each other as individuals. The more we have in common, the more we can relate to each other. Making time to get to know each other is important.

When people find things in common and acknowledge them, this creates cohesion. When they find what is different and accept this without judging the other person, this strengthens cohesion.

If this happens, trust will grow. If the opposite happens, distrust will grow. If you make judgments about me that are inaccurate and based on prejudice and false assumptions, I will distrust you. You don't know me, and your judgment is an expression of your ignorance and bias:

> "Get to know me before you judge me."

Cohesion is generated through disclosure that is open and honest:

> "I like Bob. He always lets me know how he's going, and if there is a problem I can count on him to talk about it."
>
> "I don't like Peter. I never know what's happening inside his head. It's hard to figure him out, and he sulks when he has a problem."

¶12-050 Mutuality

Mutuality involves working together for mutual benefit. If I know what you need from me to be successful in your job, and you know what I need from you for me to be successful, we have the basis for working co-operatively together. We can be mutually beneficial to each other. I will scratch your back and you will scratch mine. Sometimes what we specifically need from each other is a matter of negotiation, but just knowing what the other values and appreciates is very useful.

> In one mediation, the male manager was an enthusiastic action man. He thought fast and talked fast. He was constantly on the move, getting things done. His assistant was a slower-paced person, very thorough in her work. She valued a calm and predictable environment.
>
> Their relationship was strained, and the manager saw his assistant as resentful and moody. She saw him as insensitive and demanding. When they met in a facilitated discussion to improve their working

relationship, it became clear how different they were. One thing they had in common was a commitment to talk and explore improvement.

They talked about what made their day enjoyable and successful. The assistant wanted peace and quiet, clear information, and direction. She needed access to resources so that she could organise things well. The manager wanted successful outcomes and time to talk at the beginning of the day and the end of the day. It was also important for him to celebrate what was going well.

When they talked about what made their day disappointing and frustrating, the assistant said: unnecessary interruptions, unclear messaging, and lack of responses to emails, phone calls and texts. The manager said he didn't like frostiness and glaring looks. He didn't appreciate angry comments and silence on issues.

They agreed to start rubbing each other up the right way, and their relationship quickly improved. Their mutuality increased and within a few weeks more trust had developed between them. They were working at honouring their commitments.

How do people improve their relationships? A good basis is to improve trust, cohesion and mutuality.

Improve trust by:

- being open and honest
- making and honouring commitments.

Improve cohesion by:

- finding things in common
- respecting differences.

Improve mutuality by:

- asking for what you want and need
- delivering what we both want and need from each other.

Chapter 13

Preventing Bullying and Harassment

¶13-010 Why do people avoid bullying?

Imagine a workplace where people don't bully or harass each other. It's not a fairy tale. It is simply a workplace where people avoid using bullying and harassing behaviour.

What makes people avoid using bullying and harassing behaviour?

This is an important question because it makes us think on a personal level. What would it take for any person to choose not to bully or harass, despite having an opportunity to do so?

It is important that people know what sorts of behaviours might constitute bullying or harassment. But there is more to it than this.

When asked what would prevent them from using bullying or harassing behaviours at work, people have said:

> "I hate bullying and harassment. I wouldn't want to inflict this on anyone."
>
> "I wouldn't want people to think of me as a bully."
>
> "I value respect and believe no-one deserves to be bullied or harassed."
>
> "I wouldn't want to be bullied or harassed myself, so I don't do it to others."
>
> "It's against my values."
>
> "I believe in doing to others what you want others to do to you."

One of the things that people never say is:

> "I don't want to bully or harass because I could get into trouble."

This is interesting because many organisations attempt to demotivate people from bullying and harassing by threatening disciplinary action if they do it:

> "We will not tolerate bullying and harassment and will dismiss anyone who does it."

The threat of punishment is a very poor demotivator. Our society shows that the fear of going to prison doesn't stop many people committing crimes. Despite having Brodie's Law, which means a workplace bully might face criminal charges, people still bully in the state of Victoria, Australia. Laws don't demotivate people.

The responsibility of preventing bullying and harassment rests primarily on employers. They need to create the kind of environment that inhibits these hazards. This takes more than having a zero-tolerance policy. Preventing something is not about being intolerant of it. We don't prevent cancer by not tolerating it. We prevent it by living healthy lives, maintaining our immune systems, and getting regular check-ups so it can be detected in the early stages and addressed effectively by medical treatments.

People don't restrain their destructive impulses because they are afraid of getting caught and punished, they restrain them because they value people.

> He aha te mea nui o te ao? He tāngata, he tāngata, he tāngata.
>
> What is the most important thing in all the world? It is people, it is people, it is people.
>
> Māori whakataukī (proverb)

Interviews with people who have bullied and later reformed their behaviour provide some useful information:

- "I never really thought what I was doing was bullying. I was striving to get results and pushing people too hard. I didn't see it as bullying. I do now."
- "I felt I had a right to bully because of what I thought about the other person. In my mind at the time was they were asking for it. I blamed them for my behaviour."
- "Everyone got bullied. It happened to me as well. It was normal. No-one saw it as bullying. It was more of a lesson or a joke, or that's what we told ourselves."
- "I had a bad temper and I could hold a grudge. It was about pay-back. I thought I had a right to do what I did."
- "I grew up with the 'us and them' mentality. You were in the group or not in the group. If you were not in the group, you were seen as less worthy of respect."
- "I just never thought about what the person was suffering because of my behaviour. I didn't give it a thought. I just thought about myself."

These comments reveal that people bully and harass when they do not identify with others, and they do not understand the impact of their behaviour. In the pursuit of their own personal goals people often act without consideration.

> During a training session on bullying and harassment, a trainee spoke up in the group and said he wondered if others thought he was a bully. The facilitator responded by asking the man why he was asking the question. The man said that realised he used some of the behaviours that had been discussed and wondered what others thought about him. The facilitator asked him how he might react if others confirmed his concerns. The man said he would value others being honest with him and that he didn't

want to be thought of as a bully. The facilitator asked if the man would like others to raise their hands to indicate if they had witnessed bullying behaviour from this man. He agreed. The facilitator then asked the group to indicate their view. Everyone raised their hands. Feedback from the manager of the team two months later revealed the man had changed his behaviour because of the session.

Human beings are socially oriented. We generally want to belong. We want to be accepted and thought well of. This is an important motivator in the prevention of bullying and harassment. When a person understands that their behaviour may cause rejection, this can motivate them to change far more than the fear of punishment. Therefore, processes that create the opportunity for people to get feedback and understand how their behaviour is viewed can be very useful. Informal interventions create the opportunities for this to happen.

So how can organisations develop?

On an educational level, it requires that people understand what bullying and harassment involve in terms of behaviour. Organisations need to have regular training that is mandated under their health and safety programmes.

On a social level, team development creates positive peer pressure that encourages people to support each other and align to certain values. Those in authority need to lead by example and create clear expectations. Appraisals that focus on manager competencies in this area incentivise managers to develop their people management skills.

On a process level, organisations need to develop the capacity to resolve conflicts before they develop into bullying and harassment. Nipping things in the bud is vitally important. They need to investigate complaints when it is required and be prepared to dismiss employees regardless of how important they are. Decisive action indicates genuine commitment. In many organisations, it is not until someone is dismissed for bullying or harassment that significant change occurs throughout the workforce.

On an individual level, organisations need to encourage the development of relational empathy and build emotional intelligence. Counselling and coaching should be available to anyone who is deficient in these areas.

¶13-020 A typical prevention programme

Organisations that want to create a bullying and harassment prevention programme might consider the following strategy.

Step 1: Create a comprehensive policy for the prevention of bullying and harassment. Align this with organisational values, codes of conduct, and any other related policies. Ensure the policy is up to date and covers important features such as definition, behavioural examples, informal and formal options, who to talk to in the initial stages, false complaints, and other relevant information.

Step 2: Start by training managers. They need to be equipped before staff receive training so they can address issues that might be raised after the training. Consider the development of senior managers who can investigate complaints, as well as those who can provide specific informal interventions.

Step 3: Choose and train contact persons for their role as a "first point of contact" so that they can assist people who raise issues.

Step 4: Train health and safety representatives, union delegates, and others who might be approached by employees.

Step 5: Commence training all staff. Small group training appears to have the best outcomes. Facilitators and trainers should be selected who can provide a safe environment where people can discuss bullying and harassment issues. This group-centred training should be refreshed every three or four years.

Step 6: Provide eLearning modules for staff and managers that are easily accessible and can be rolled out on a yearly basis, so there is a record of training.

Step 7: Collect data from surveying, exit interviews, and the contact person programme (confidentiality is required).

A prevention programme needs to be regularly supported and assessed, instead of relying on a single, isolated training event.

¶13-030 Contact person programmes

It is important to have people within organisations that staff can talk to about bullying and harassment. Managers can do this, but people don't often want to approach a manager. Employment assistance programme counsellors can do this, but they are outside the workplace. A contact person is someone at work who can be approached confidentially and is trained to assist enquirers as a first point of contact.

The contact person's role is to:

- listen to concerns about bullying and harassment with empathy and understanding
- provides information about the organisation's policy and options for resolving issues
- support a person to make their own decisions
- maintain confidentiality.

People often talk to contact persons because they are discreet, have useful information, and most of all are peers who are credible.

Contact persons are usually a mixture of staff and managers. They should not be union delegates, because this clashes with their advocacy role. Union delegates may receive the training, but it is important to ensure there is not a conflict of interest. Contact persons are not advocates and do not get actively involved in resolution processes.

Contact persons do not have authority to act in a disciplinary way. They are not workplace police and should take a manager's role. Therefore, contact persons should not be referred to as "officers". This term has sometimes been used, but it sends the wrong message about the role of contact persons.

Contact Persons should be nominated and chosen rather than being open to volunteers. Sometimes people who aspire to be contact persons can be dangerous if they cannot keep matters confidential or if they get too involved with people's concerns. Contact persons should be nominated by staff and managers on the following criteria:

- They can be discreet and maintain confidentiality. They do not gossip.
- They have good standing with their teams. They should not be people who bully or harass, and they should not be irresponsible.
- They are good listeners and genuinely care about people.

Contact persons should receive specific training that gives them the knowledge required to be useful. They also need skills to listen effectively so they can quickly engage and assist a person who may be shocked, confused, distrustful, anxious, sad or angry. They also require ongoing support and skill development. The contact person programme should receive a short refresher on a yearly basis.

Contact persons need to be accountable and relate to the others and the coordinator of the programme. This ensures they don't become "lone rangers" who are doing their own thing. They need to be under a contract and managed by the coordinator of the programme. They may need to be removed if they break confidentiality or show they cannot be trusted in the role.

The main value of contact person programmes is that they provide early intervention and therefore offer the possibility of a resolution at the lowest level necessary. Without this, bullying and harassment issues become more complex and disruptive.

> Brian asked to meet with a contact person. Initially he was angry about a colleague he had conflict with. Since then, they had both avoided each other, but Brian had come to learn that his colleague was bad-mouthing him behind his back. Brian wanted to make a complaint but thought it would be useful to talk to a contact person first.
>
> Brian initially expressed his anger and explained that he was going to make a complaint about his colleague, but as the contact person engaged with him, his anger reduced and he became more reflective. Instead of

> making a formal complaint, Brian spoke with his manager and requested an informal intervention. This resulted in a facilitated discussion where Brian and his colleague agreed on a way forward that was managed and monitored by the manager.

Contact persons can operate as a force for resolution by taking the heat out of situations and assisting people to resolve issues. However, to do this, contact persons need to be selected, trained, managed, and supported.

¶13-040 Training sessions

The best type of staff training on bullying and harassment involves sessions that are facilitated so that people can contribute their knowledge and experience. Most people have a story about bullying or harassment, and trainees often learn a lot from each other, as well as from the trainer.

However, to achieve this kind of training experience, facilitators need to be able to create an environment that is safe and secure. Talking about bullying and harassment in a group can be threatening to some people, and this will usually cause them to either shut down and disengage or try to control the group and the facilitator.

> In one staff training session, a participant began to shake. He looked down and could not speak when asked questions. The session stopped and the facilitator took him aside. He discovered the trainee had been previously bullied and suffered from post-traumatic stress disorder. The session had been too much for him to engage in, and he was unable to continue.

> In another staff training session, a participant started by accusing the management of covering up bullying matters. He expressed anger and began to challenge the facilitator. The facilitator managed to relate to the expression of anger without escalating the situation. He transformed the situation so that it was beneficial to the participant as well as the group.

Facilitators need to be competent to work with displays of emotion and defensiveness in sessions. They need to show respect for everyone and be able to work with the group to create a shared learning experience. Facilitated sessions not only provide information about the subject matter and the organisation's policy but they provide for the development of cohesion, as people will share their thoughts, experiences and feelings.

Well-facilitated sessions will build cohesion and trust. They also build a common commitment from the people participating:

> I want to ask for a commitment from each of you as we finish the session today: firstly, that you look at yourself and your own behaviour and make sure you don't bully or harass anyone, and secondly, that you

don't turn a blind eye to it if you witness it happening to someone else. Who can make that commitment today?

To create a learning culture in a training session it is important for the facilitator to connect with each person present. The initial disclosures should be valued, and the facilitator should interact with each person to build cohesion and trust.

Facilitators should start by clarifying the purpose of the session and giving a brief description of the content:

> We are here to look at two very common hazards that damage people and workplaces: workplace bullying and harassment. Our organisation has a responsibility under various laws to prevent these hazards from harming people. Part of that is to have training, so everyone knows some important things:
>
> - What is bullying or harassment and what isn't?
> - How are these terms defined legally?
> - How do they affect people and the culture of an organisation?
> - What can people do if they experience bullying or harassment?
> - What can we all do to prevent these hazards from occurring?

It is useful and helpful to establish some group rules. This lets people know how to conduct themselves in the training session.

Typical group rules:

- Don't bully or harass anyone in the group.
- Don't defame anyone or accuse people in or outside the group.
- Respect other people's right to their opinions – don't force your opinion on them.
- Allow people to speak without interrupting them.
- Don't repeat anything that anyone says of a personal nature. Share any information you learn but not the personal stories that people share.

Attending to the purpose and culture of a group is important to create a safe environment. This involves setting some boundaries about behaviour and will make it easier for people to talk openly and engage. It is important that the facilitator does not try and pressure people to divulge their personal history of bullying and harassment. This will cause people to shut down instead. However, a good facilitator will "warm people up" to expressing themselves and gently encourage openness and empathy in the group:

> I would like to begin by asking you to think about your experience of bullying or harassment. You may have been the target of it in the past. You may have witnessed it happening to others and been affected by

> that. You may have even done some of it yourself in the past. I have been in each of these categories myself. I have been the target and there have been times when I have been the perpetrator. So, share as much as you feel comfortable with sharing today. Your input may be helpful to others. Let's go around the room and spend some time hearing from each of you. Let people know something that you know about bullying or harassment. Who wants to start?

A good facilitator will monitor the mood or dynamics occurring in a group. Sometimes people speak up with enthusiasm, and sometimes people seem reluctant and quiet. It can be helpful to ask someone to start, especially if someone appears ready to speak:

> John, you look like you have something to say.

In a small group this beginning phase might take an hour, but it is valuable. People engage with each other in a way that is unifying and mutually beneficial. Once this engagement has occurred, people will contribute more and more, and the facilitator will create a rich learning environment that people will remember and value.

This is different than attending a lecture. This kind of facilitated session creates a deep experience and assists in developing a caring and preventative culture.

¶13-050 A final word

Bullying and harassment can happen in any workplace. They will most likely happen in every workplace. This is inevitable because people learn to bully and harass in families, in schools, and in societal groups. These people also get jobs, and they enter workplaces where they interact with others. They bring their behaviour with them.

Organisations can do a lot to prevent bullying and harassment from occurring and continuing to occur in their workplaces. They should, given their legal responsibilities, take action to eliminate bullying and harassment, and this begins by identifying what bullying and harassment behaviour is, educating their employees sufficiently, and providing effective processes to address issues when they arise. More than this, they can create and maintain a culture that is healthy and cohesive.

This is a challenge for twenty-first century organisations, but the costs of allowing bullying and harassment to occur are too high to ignore. Bullying and harassment are destructive forms of behaviour. They are bad for people. They are bad for business. Preventing bullying and harassment is the responsibility of every employer and employee.

Made in United States
Orlando, FL
05 November 2026

90230605R00081